Outside Directors in the Family Owned Business

Why, When, Who and How

Léon A. Danco
Donald J. Jonovic

Post Office Box 24268
Cleveland, Ohio 44124

Library of Congress Cataloging in Publication Data

Danco, Léon A., 1923-
  Outside directors in the family company

  Includes index.
    1. Family corporations—Management. 2. Directors of
corporations.   I. Jonovic, Donald J.   II. Title
HD62.25.D36   658.4'22   81-12931
ISBN 0-9603614-3-X   AACR2

©1981 The University Press, Inc.

Third Printing: November 1987

Printed USA

Table of Contents

Acknowledgement

To publish this book without recognizing the debt we owe to the outside directors of The Center for Family Business—past and present—would be unthinkable.

Over the past 20 years, their contribution to us and our company has been beyond measure—both in giving us the tools to solve our problems and in helping us to assure our own future. We are deeply grateful to them and want, here, to acknowledge the benefit we have received through their example and commitment to us.

The thoughts expressed in this book reflect both our experience as advocates of the use of outside directors, as well as our good fortune to be personal beneficiaries of their contribution. With our directors, and through their support, we have evolved many of the ideas discussed in this book—concepts

1

and practices which have proven invaluable, not only to us, but to all the many families in business whom we know to have followed our example and our suggestions.

Léon A. Danco

Introduction

Contrary to popular opinion, America's family-owned and privately held corporations are not being destroyed by confiscatory taxation, runaway inflation, ruthless competitors, unproductive labor, technological change, insidious regulation, or even the presumed decline in the work ethic among the young.

These are just a few of the more common scapegoats blamed for the untimely demise of so many once thriving businesses—but these are not the *underlying* reasons. These businesses fail because they have allowed themselves to be destroyed, slowly but surely, by the actions—or more accurately the inactions, the inattention, and the irresponsibility—of their boards of directors, the very bodies who are charged by law with the protection and survival of the businesses they "direct."

More often than not, the decisions needed to assure the viability of family businesses in an ever more complex world are never made. Why? Because the typical American director is unqualified to hold his—or her—job, that's why.

If you don't believe this, consider who the directors of America's corporations really are. Excepting as statistically insignificant the 100-200 thousand or so "professional" directors who inhabit the boardrooms of our relatively well-known publicly owned companies, we find that the 3-4 *million* directors of the 1.5 million privately held, family owned, and owner-managed corporations are mostly *non* -directors.

Yet these non-directors are the people who, by law, are supposedly responsible for the economic policies of profit-making organizations whose combined output represents nearly half of our gross national product. Their decisions and actions affect close to half of all American workers—those who are employed by the so-called "small business" community.

And what is the most common occupation among these millions of mostly inappropriate, but legally elected corporate directors? Motherhood, in case you didn't already guess—but Momma's not alone. More often than not, the boardrooms of America's privately owned businesses are also home to a mixed bag of Rasputins, advisors on retainer, some grateful old-time managers, the little old lady with a moustache who keeps the books, the widow of Dad's old partner, a retired dentist (who invested a few extra dollars when the company was founded), and an assortment of brothers, sisters and cousins who are generally hostile.

Sometimes, even, The Boss puts one of his kids on the board to "learn." The Kid also serves the coffee.

At best, this kind of board will supply silence and agreement to the owner-manager, who, also at best, considers them a damn nuisance. Or, he uses his board as a cheap ("no fee, just dinner") way to reward faithful, dependent ("unquestioning") relatives or grateful ("scared") employees.

He also realizes the board's value in lulling hostile minority shareholders into thinking they know what's going on.

These are rubber stamp, pseudo-boards, ready collections of "yes" men, controlled by owner-managers who hold most—if not all—of the chips. These "directors" rarely offer any constructive criticism, they don't have much to say—if they say anything at all—and they mostly approve, willingly or unwillingly, whatever The Boss says to approve.

The Boss says: "Charlie, sign here." Charlie says: "What for?" The Boss says: "Never mind, just sign..." And Charlie signs—over and over again.

Such an extension of The Boss's ego doesn't often even require a meeting. Meetings are legally mandated, but in too many cases they're neither formal nor real. They can even consist of nothing more than the company attorney overseeing the writing of minutes to meetings that were never held, just to make sure everything is properly and legally recorded in the event the IRS wants to scrutinize the "legitimacy" of any decisions or deductions.

Such "boards" as these are useless, at best. At worst, they're destructive because they provide either:

a) A stamp of justification to the business owner's ever-growing sense of "divine right," which has too often resulted in some catastrophic judgements—or

b) A continuing arena where bitterness, greed, envy, and "entitlement" tend to demolish any semblance of long-term objective planning, making sure everyone forgets the necessity to avoid gutting the goose that lays the golden eggs.

Such "boards" deny the chief executive any forum wherein he can honestly express his hopes, his fears, his concerns, and his doubts before other human beings whom he believes can help him resolve his difficulties.

It's terrible to have no place to go for help when you're really alone...and scared.

If a business owner wants to get together with his management, he can hold a staff meeting and tell them what he wants (is going?) to do—after all, he is their boss. If he wants opinions from friends or relatives, he can invite them over for dinner, hold a bridge party, or rent the club for an evening. If he wants the opinions of his advisors, all he has to do is ask them— and, of course, pay them. If the hostile minority shareholders feel they are entitled to a "voice," they can ask for formalized shareholders meetings—leaving the board and its business to directors interested in more than just upholding their own dividends, benefits, and prejudices.

Too often, though, these staff/family/advisor/investor meetings are combined under the name of a *board* meeting, and, thus, one of the most potentially powerful tools for making sure the company continues, grows, and stays healthy in these complex times is thrown away.

OUTSIDERS ARE NEEDED

No well-run business, family-owned or not, can operate efficiently over any extended period of time without a periodic review of both the actions of its executive officers and the policies they pursue to meet the challenge of the future. And the body best designed to deliver this review is the board of directors.

Yet, instead of setting up such a reviewing body, the business owner—if he has his way—generally packs his "court" with shills (whose opinions are too often just what he wants to hear—and when), and if some of his "directors" by accident prove troublesome, he can always schedule irrelevant dog and pony shows to silence criticism or disagreement.

This controlled world might reinforce The Beleaguered Boss's desire for control or flexibility, but his comfort is temporary. Sooner or later, he will learn that no owner-manager—no matter how competant or successful he is in the short run—can go it alone forever. It's great to be independent, but loneliness is a heavy price to pay for the privilege. The fate of an economic athiest is the same as that of a spiritual athiest. After he goes, there is nothing.

A successful founder's company is not so much a family or closely held corporation, as it is a *custom built corporation* . It's his, and his alone, and it's carefully, painfully designed to fit his impressive (if unique) frame.

But if his business is going to survive, the founder must someday learn to recut that well-tailored suit to fit the *next* generation of managers, who must survive in *their* economic times. This is something he finds next to impossible to do or even contemplate.

The founder of a successful business is a lonely architect. There are no codes or regulations telling him how to design his business. If he manages to succeed after years of expecting the whole thing to collapse about him, in his surprise and relief he almost inevitably begins to enshrine what he did to get there. He has to. It's all he knows. He begins to manage by superstition, like the paratrooper who pats his favorite pin-up's fanny before every jump. If he survives he assumes it's thanks to her pretty little butt. Don't ever try to tell him it was the parachute—or even his training.

While he was so busily spending the past 20 to 30 years building his business, the world was just as busily changing. He knows little about that, though, because his survival depended on tunnel vision, a single-minded dedication to one goal—the survival and growth of his business.

A business founder usually has very specific—and very considerable—talents as an engineer, technician, salesman, designer, or operator. These talents enabled him to succeed, but at a considerable price—the business founder lives, thinks, and dreams alone. He lives a managerially celibate life locked away in a corporate monastary.

For this reason, even though a business owner may be "successful" in the short term (after all, he *is* alive, and he *has* made money), he is typically a lousy long-term manager. His

talents—which are immense—are usually confined to a few
narrow bands of activity. This is comfortable for him—like an old
pair of shoes—and his rubber stamp board is little more than an
added cushion between him and the street.

THE OBJECTIVE VIEWPOINT

Most owner-managers believe they get enough
stimulation from their sporadic meetings with assorted
customers, suppliers, competitors, advisors, and employees. They
have fictional boards with whistle-stop meetings and pseudo-
directors. They think they get too *much* , let alone enough,
advice. But they are wrong. These business owners are mistaking
a series of casual affairs for true commitment.

A board is like a marriage. It's a necessary institution for a
given way of life. Nothing guarantees that it has to work out well.
Like marriage, however, it does provide the formal setting in
which people who dream together can build something together.

Every president needs others to help him do his job,
people with whom he can be open and honest, people whom he
can respect and who respect him, and people who, he feels, are
committed to his dream.

Every conscientious president needs a competent,
working board of outside directors to serve as his challenger,
supporter, and enforcer, as well as his conceptualizer, arbiter,
and monitor.

This kind of board *can* be a yardstick by which the chief
executive *can* measure himself, his goals, his responsibilities, and
his actions. It *can* serve as a kind of professional association where
he *can* exchange views with his peers. It *can* give him moral
support and an opportunity for discussion, decision, and action.

This book is about such directors. It's about such working
boards and their roles in family companies. It's about a concept
we have been recommending to successful business owners for
two decades. We have seen the creation of many hundreds of
such working boards of qualified outside directors and we have

seen the benefits they can bring.

But such boards cannot and do not exist except in companies where the owner manager, himself, desires that they exist. They are the result of a business owner's recognition that he cannot do the really important things alone.

It's *not* intended however, that a board act as a substitute for holding meaningful discussions with your advisors. Its purpose, instead, is to act as a catalyst for such discussions.

It's *not* intended that a board replace top-level management meetings held with your key people. It's intended, instead, to help you realize both the true talents and the real limits of your key managers.

It's *not* intended that a board will help you escape from some bloody fights with hostile relatives, partners, and other disgruntled shareholders. We can hope, though, that a board will help you realize the error of some of your earlier decisions, will help you realize that some price is always paid for privilege, and will help you make the hard personal decisions you know you have to make.

It surely is *not* intended that these following chapters serve as a textbook for amateur do-it-yourselfers. Rather, it's intended to act as an encouragement to you to come together with contributory accountants, attorneys, bankers, planners, insurance agents, or other advisors, to ask for (and accept) the benefit of their expertise in helping you create such a working board for you and your company.

And a board is *not* a panacea. It won't eliminate problems, but it can help you find solutions.

The successful owner-manager must accept the fact that he needs objective review from competent, compassionate outsiders to ensure *his* security and *his* survival—as well as that of the company he helped build.

Those readers who adamantly refuse to concede that there might be some merit to this opinion might as well put this book down right now.

Sure there are lots of concerns raised by the creation of a true *working* board—and some valid caveats—but for the most part, business owners' fears about boards come from the same source as old wives' tales—the fables and fantasies of people who have little or no relevant experience, and very little faith in themselves.

From our experiences and observations, the very concept of a useful, contributory board is usually either overlooked, ignored, or unknown until brought up in a positive way. Regardless of what they say, business owners—successful and otherwise—don't refuse to have a working board of directors for economic, legal, competitive, or any other such imagined constraint. *They don't have 'em because they don't want 'em— even though what they say is that they don't need 'em.*

We haven't simply been observers of this subject. We've been *participants* in it. After 20 years and countless thousands of discussions with untold numbers of business owners and their families, we've developed an understanding of the "gut" issues that are involved in decisions to have—or not to have—an outside board. With that understanding, and with the commitment of clients and prospective directors, we've succeeded beyond all expectations in the creation of such boards.

We've written this book, therefore, as a straightforward discussion of why business owners should consider having a real board of working outside directors, and what to do with them once they're in place. *For without the business owner's desire to create such a board, he will have no useful board .*

This book addresses the subject as we've lived it. Its style and content reflect the temperament of the business owners (a) as we have met them, (b) as we have struggled with them to overcome their overwhelming tendencies to reject review because "my business is different, my family is different, my needs are different," and (c) as we have succeeded in convincing them.

So let us explore, together, the nature of family-owned companies themselves, as well as the structure of their typical boards—as they mostly exist, and as they mostly fail. Without this understanding, it would be impossible to determine *why* a working board is appropriate, *when* the time is right to creat one, *who* would qualify as objective, competent outsiders, and *how* , first, to go about creating a board, second, to use it for everyone's benefit, and, thirdly, to enjoy having it around.

Incidentally, while most founders to date can be most accurately called "Old Dad" (rather than "Old Mom"), the inheritor/successors in the next generation of a family business will surely be both female as well as male. Daughters, as inheritor/ successor-managers, will be increasingly more common in the years to come. (Less and less will they act only through their husbands, the son-in- law whom Old Dad always regards as the gorilla in bed with his daughter, the guy to whom Dad never gave any stock for fear that he might someday leave his baby and take the company.) Daughters-in-law, too, those women who marry the Boss's sons, are increasingly having a voice in the management of their husbands companies.

Every day, widows and sisters of owners are increasingly becoming active in the continuing managment of the business created by the founders. In the years to come, women will/must fill an increasing number of CEO slots in successful family-owned businesses if the continuity of those companies is to be assured. The increasing role of women as executives and CEO's is one of the most fascinating changes on the business horizon.

But the English language does not adjust easily to such changes in social reality. It's our intention that all references to Dad, son, man, him, his, he, and Charlie, be taken as equally referring to Mom, daughter, woman, her, hers, she, and Mary—and vice versa. There is no reason half of our population should feel slighted, ignored, or relegated to a secondary position simply because the English language is so poorly equipped to express ideas which are neutral in gender. At the outset, therefore, we beg the forebearance and forgiveness of any among our readers who might otherwise feel left out or neglected. You are very much in our minds, if not in our speech.

WE CAN HELP EACH OTHER

People who could qualify as outside directors for successful family companies are relatively rare, that's true. But there *are* enough of them around to fill the needs of those who are fortunate enough to recognize their value. Finding them, however, requires knowing who they are and where to look for them. Therefore, we invite any reader who is interested in either (a) creating an outside board for himself, or (b) participating as a director on the boards of others, to please contact us.

We would also welcome hearing from those of you who have already created boards with outside directors, or who already serve in that capacity with a successful family business. We hope you will share your ideas and experiences with us.

To live with a working board of outside directors is to participate in an ever-changing forum, to deal with new ideas, new challenges, and new directions in our ever more complex world. As one CEO told us just recently as he was reflecting on his first year with such a board, "I'm not so scared anymore...and it's not so lonely as it used to be.. I'm really excited, now, about facing the future."

His experience isn't unique. Each of us needs all the help he can find.

Léon A. Danco

Section I

Who Needs An Outside Board Anyway?

Chapter 1

Inside Boards and How They Grew

Every family corporation has a board of directors, because boards are required by law.

But the fact that every family corporation has a board doesn't mean that these boards *direct* anything. Most family business boards are lucky if they *meet*, much less direct.

We've even found directors who didn't know they were directors. At a recent seminar attended by business owners and their spouses, for example, one couple divided up their introduction of themselves in the traditional way. Dad talked about the business. Mom talked about the kids.

This business owner explained that he had 40 employees, did $2.8 million in volume, served a statewide area, and that the board of directors he had since the beginning consisted of himself (of course), his attorney, and his wife.

His wife then described their family and her role as "housewife and production manager of the next generation." After a brief pause, she looked down at her seated, smiling husband and said:

"I also just found out that I've been a director of our company for the past 20 years."

THE TYPICAL INSIDE BOARD

Why should she know? The board didn't do anything. Like most boards of family-owned businesses, it consisted of The Boss (who ran the show), Momma (who stayed out of the way), and the Scribe, (who wrote the minutes of meetings that never took place).

Most business owners have no intention of packing *their* boardrooms with smart-alecs, second-guessers, and critics. They're much more comfortable with having the necessary signatures supplied by willing and unquestioning hands, while leaving the creation of IRS-inspired meeting minutes to the Scribe.

The business owner's relationship to his board is usually something on the order of "I do the directing—you just sign." So, to fill the requirements of the law, instead of holding genuine, useful meetings, he turns an otherwise first class attorney into a second-class novelist writing imaginary scenarios.

Membership on these inside boards can become a lot more complicated than just Momma, the Scribe, and The Boss. As time goes by, and the cast taking part in the family business spectacle expands, the plot tends to thicken.

If Old Dad took on investors in the early days ("...with *your* money and *my* brains..."), they considered themselves "silent" partners. Dad gave them a seat on the board so they could be fooled into thinking they had some control over their investment. A lot of relatives and dentists get board seats this way.

As time passes, Dad usually discovers that a board seat is also a good (cheaper than a raise) way to reward his faithful employees for their loyalty (compliance). They stuck with him through all the disasters, potential disasters, and knuckle-whiteners of the early days. He wants them to know he hasn't forgotten.

A board seat can also be an excellent way to "promote" a restless key manager, giving him only a little increase in pay and no increase in authority.

And speaking of pay—what a clever way "directors' fees" can be for getting money to the family pre-tax. Make Uncle Charlie a director, and the fees will help support his convalescence. Sons (and daughters) can always use some ready cash, and surely sons-in-law can use their fees to support the grandchildren in ways to which their grandfather wants them to become accustomed.

And how about the sons who are working out of town in the branch offices? Making them directors is a good way to give them more prestige, both at home and in the field, without any real power to screw things up.

What better way for the entire family to appreciate the whole operation than attending board meetings—held in "relaxing" environments, 1500 miles from home?

(Woe betide anybody who steps out of bounds, however, and questions the decisions or policies of The Boss. That's the surest way for a grateful director to become an ungrateful ex-director.)

Assuming that we can keep any hostilities from surfacing, or any antagonists from being seated, inside boards are pure corporate theater.

MINUTES TO MEETINGS NEVER HELD

Even though all these people might take their "directorships" very seriously and expect to meet once in a while, for the most part these meetings, too, are rarely held. The Boss's major goal, after all, is to make sure important subjects don't ever come up in the presence of people who could ask embarrassing questions.

Still, meetings are all duly recorded in the "minutes," usually written long after the fact, mainly for providing "substantiation." Except for the occasional IRS agent's prying eyes, however, the contents of these minutes are mostly ignored throughout the normal course of events...and rightly so.

As time continues to pass, and as some businesses succeed beyond their owners' fondest earlier expectations, some of the resulting extra (pre-tax) cash ends up funding directors meetings held in increasingly exotic places. Meetings are more frequently scheduled at luxurious resorts in the sun. If not in The Islands, then some nice stateside spa, usually different each time. Wherever held, however, the family business "board meetings" now tend to become deductible junkets and sources of applause for the owner-manager/CEO/chairman. Potentially questioning mouths are kept full with a steady parade of canapes and fancy tropical drinks.

Afterwards, the well-fed and well-lubricated Scribe heads back to his office, pulls some canned boilerplate out of his word-processing files, and composes the "minutes" of what was essentially a cocktail/dinner/beach party.

If the company was co-founded by several more or less "equal partners," the most likely result is that just the investors make up the board. Board meetings in these companies too often take on the function of shareholder meetings, whose sole purpose is to rearrange company earnings into tax-free benefits of all kinds (in rather direct proportion to ownership interests, of course). It's amazing to see how creative investor/managers can get. This is called "breaking even" higher and higher.

Sometimes, however, contribution as a manager and percentage of ownership don't coincide. In these circumstances, the meetings get more acrimonious as managerial reward and ownership entitlement collide over perqs, or opportunities for the kids, or time off the job—any number of issues involving a disastrous difference of opinion about what's "fair."

The usual outcome is for the partners to dwindle in number as the stronger/smarter/more ruthless/more fertile buy/force out the interests of the weaker/less talented/less ruthless/less fertile. The ultimate survivor structure now operates with a single voice—but not necessarily with any more ability to survive into the next generation.

A "surviving" partner is often times more powerful than a solitary founder.

THE "BOARD" THE KIDS INHERIT

Eventually, however, Old Dad moves on into the Land of the Eternally Positive Cash Flow. Assuming he's been lucky enough to have some successor-managers, he includes in his "legacy" to them this fantastic collection of relatives, friends, co-conspiritors, self-servers, grateful employees, and hostile minority shareholders. Officially, it continues to be called a board, but the successors will have varying names for it in private, depending on the situation.

If majority ownership (and, therefore, control) is in the hands of a single successor, not much changes on the surface. He replaces Dad on the board, but the rest of them...The Boss's old retinue of performing (and non-performing) courtiers...hang on. Even the most fortunate inheritor, however, will eventually be heir to an additional legacy— *the problems intrinsic to working with such an inherited board* .

Among the many questions these successor-managers will eventually face are:

*Can they—and if so how do they—go about cleaning house to get some support for their plans?

*How can they persuade their widowed mother that she's no longer needed as a director of the company she and Dad built together?

*How can they move those grateful senior employees off the board without destroying their gratitude and motivation, especially now that the major guarantor of their continued tenure—the founder—has left the field?

*How can they change attorneys or accountants or bankers or any other advisors when they sit on the board?

*How can they get a replacement for Dad's old secretary now that she's secretary-treasurer/director of the corporation—and has kept the *real* minutes in her own special shorthand nobody else can read?

And these questions are only the beginning.

But if you think these are problems, remember that few successors are the only children their parents produced. If the poor, miserable successor to a founder happens to face the additional discomfort of multiple inheritors/successors, retired employees, working and non-working owners, and other assorted minority shareholders remaining from Dad's regime (none of whom ever did trust The Kid), we begin—with the arrival of the second generation—to see a lot of change in the tenor of the board meetings.

As examples: how does the successor tell his sister that, as much as he loves her, she doesn't need to be on the board to make sure her brother doesn't dip into the till—nor does she need her husband there to keep her company? How can he get competent company officers to contribute useful ideas for the benefit of the company without inviting pork barreling reciprocity among conflicting interests? How can he respond to company needs without being considered self-serving? It goes on...

...and it gets worse.

Meetings now start getting deadly serious—even though the directors still avoid such "mundane" subjects as "market direction" or "management strategy under changing conditions. " The most likely topics of discussion remain those that deal with the multitude of special interests and privileges which the "directors" assume accrue to them inexhaustibly and by entitlement/divine right because of their ownership.

Board meetings in these circumstances too often become continuing family/investor fights, usually concentrated on the self-serving issues of salaries, dividends, benefits and personalities.

At least under Dad's reign this pseudo-board didn't really absorb any management time or attention. *Now, as the successor's board, it not only doesn't "direct," it becomes a major energy dilutant, diverting sorely needed attention from vital business issues to what, essentially, are family matters .*

What's worse, all of this assumes that there is, in fact, a designated and trained successor-manager/CEO. If Dad was unlucky enough to meet his Maker without having a successor or a succession plan in place, the game is just about over. The one body—the board—that could have held the company together by using its formal authority to install a new management team, will have neither the inclination nor the ability to do so. The usual answer is a sellout—or, worse, liquidation.

The world, of course, will blame this failure on the younger generation.

WHY REAL DIRECTORS MAKE THE BOSS NERVOUS

Why does a business owner allow his company's future to get into such a sorry state? Whatever the answer, there's no question that he does. We've found over and over again that in any collection of business owners, less than one out of 20 will have on their boards directors who are truly competent outsiders. And of that small percentage, only a few (one out of 10) will have a *majority* of such objective outsiders.

Based on observations over two decades with many tens of thousands of businesses, we've concluded that *less than one family-owned, privately held company out of 200 has, out of its own instinctive sense of need, created and used a working board consisting of a majority of contributory outside directors* .

Why? Because successful entrepreneurs learn to worship "flexibility/freedom" more than almost anything else, including (it would seem) survival itself.

When business founders are feeling particularly heroic, they tend to praise freedom as one of the major blessings of being in business for themselves. And by "freedom," they usually mean the flexibility inherent in being their own boss with *no one* in a position to tell them *what* to do...or *when* ...or *why.*

Entrepreneurs even define themselves as flexible. When asked to list the major benefits of business ownership, business owners will invariably list such "advantages" as:

> " *Entrepreneurs need the flexibility to get things done. Delegation limits this ...*"
> "*... having control within a limited number of shareholders is great because it avoids the requirement to make reports to the public or anybody else. There's no harrassment.* "
> " *If I want to do something, I don't have to take a Gallup Poll. I'm flexible. I can act.* "
> " *Etc...etc...* "

The primary law in the family business universe says: *Whoever owns the majority of the stock has the power and the perogative to make all of the decisions* . As one fellow put it to us in a seminar a few years ago, "Happiness is control." In fact, one of the main advantages of being in business for yourself is working to no standards other than your own.

Entrepreneurs are facinated by this Utopian concept of Freedom from Judgement. Many of them even think it's one of the great values of life, and preserve this "freedom" right to the end—which inevitably comes.

The trouble with a real board is it can look a little too much like a "boss." And who wants that?

Don't get us wrong. In its place, flexibility *is* a great thing. Think back. Remember the days when we'd play sandlot ball as kids, the days when the one-man play was the rule? It had to be. Nobody knew any others. Everybody played mainly for the fun and competition—rules, tactics, review, practice just got in the way of having fun. That was real flexibility, real satisfaction.

Most of us, in fact, can play sandlot ball year after year—and have a good time doing it—without any serious problems. But for those who become professionals, the story's a lot different. While an amateur can maintain his freedom to run all over the field, the professional game requires organization. A successful family business is a "professional" game, not a sandlot exercise. It needs all the professionalism it can get if it is to survive as a complex organization in a complex world.

In the beginning, a business founder could afford to avoid discipline and systems because he was playing for personal survival. He learned a new profession—business owner—and (on most days) had a lot of fun doing so. "Flexibility" was really his disorganized way of accentuating action at the expense of organization or planning.

But as the business grows, planning becomes more important to corporate survival (even to "breaking even...higher and higher"). Things are no longer so simple. There are so many more people, products, competitors, rules, customers, and dollars to think about. Even "success" becomes harder to define. It used to be a good day when a few bucks were left over in the till, but, eventually, bureaucratic terms such as "cash flow," "margin," "return on investment," "market analysis," "strategic planning," "management development," and the like start popping up. Those become the measures of results, and they require organization in order to work.

Even in the face of all this, the business owner remains convinced that any attempt at "organization" cramps his flexibility. Therefore, because the desire for flexibility was one of the major reasons the founder went into business for himself in the first place, organization is the development he resists the most.

There are *many* formalities the business owner tends to resist. He seldom holds meetings of his advisors as a group. He seldom meets, as a group, with shareholders, with his employees, or even with his family to discuss the opportunities and needs of the business in the years to come. He seldom takes the time to draw and maintain an up-to-date, accurate organization chart. He avoids writing down well-defined job descriptions or a well-understood succession plan which follows measurable criteria.

There are a lot of things he doesn't do.

Because all these actions would limit the business owner's beloved "flexibility," he resists them. In fact, he organizes his entire business to make it nearly impossible to build any fences around his pasture. Small wonder he resists any attempt to create a board of objective outside directors, and listens with approval to horror stories about what happened to those who did, or to those people who say, "You don't need one."

An objective outside board is needed as a way of putting either constructive restraints or rational support around the unbounded "flexibility" inherent in business ownership. It's a way of getting constructive reviewers in to watch the game and the players so that some consistent outcomes can be planned. But because business owners tend to equate being "reviewed" with being "bossed," all too few family businesses have real boards.

WHY "FLEXIBILITY" IS DANGEROUS

There's another good reason for "flexibility." It lets The Boss take advantage of good fortune, with the extra bonus that He won't have to admit His plans failed if it turns out He was wrong.

Why else do you think he hangs onto his secrecy? He may have had really good reasons to be secretive in the beginning ("If they knew how bad things are..."), but as his business grows, he stays secretive to stay "flexible." After all, if he doesn't announce his plans to anyone, he knows how easy it will be to change them.

Secrecy, however, is an overvalued luxury, one that becomes less and less affordable as the founder's business and business family grow. Sooner or later, in fact, it becomes downright dangerous.

No matter how much he'd like to maintain his amateur status, success eventually forces the founder to become a professional. His business ceases being a game, or even a profitable hobby, and becomes more and more an institution with a life of its own. And running an institution requires formality (which is too often confused with "rigidity").

But as long as the business owner wants full freedom, autonomy, and a lack of review, he can use his power to maintain a non-functioning or rubber stamp pseudo-board.

And it *is* his prerogative. *Nothing or nobody requires the formation of a working board. It only comes about if the owner manager desires effective help to ensure the long-term viability of his company—and this requires outside directors who can stand up to the business owner's flak long enough to given him the advice, support, and help he needs .*

The business owner is the key. *Only he can make himself ready to chair an objective outside board,* and the only way he can do this is by seriously reflecting on his own history and on his own needs.

The problem, of course, is that the characteristics that make for success in the early days render most business owners totally unreceptive to the demands of the job of Chairman of the Board. There are few aspects of their personalities that predispose them to asking—much less accepting—the help and advice of others.

Everybody knows the entrepreneurial legends. Dad's "war stories" are probably as firmly entrenched in family and business lore as ghosts in Halloween tradition. But let's take a closer look.

WHY THE BOSS MAKES HIS MISTAKES

The making of a successful business owner is a high-temperature, high-pressure process, which uses the raw material of his *talent* (the founder's unique genius), *resources* (his health, his experience, his friends—and mostly other people's money), and his *time* (which is limited) to seize an opportunity he sees.

The successful founder is a winner who emerges shaken and scarred from a crowd full of losers. He gets his MBA in Survival, working with little else on his side other than Sweat Equity and an understanding spouse.

In the entrepreneur's early years, there is no "balance" in the balance sheet, no "income" in the income statement. The profit and loss statement is half misnamed. His survival depends on one management theory: if it works, do it. If it doesn't, do something else...quick.

This is the time when our CEO-to-be learns to play everything close to his chest. This is the time he learns that usually the only person he can trust or depend on for anything is himself. Early on, the business founder taught himself to be especially careful what he told anybody about his business—he learned to be secretive and lonely.

He knows if he told the bank how bad things were, they'd call the loan. He knows if he told his suppliers how bad things were, they'd demand cash up front. He knows if the word got out, the employees would quit, Momma would demand that he get a real job, and—worst of all—his in-laws would have been right all along.

So he says nothing to nobody...nohow...never. It becomes a sacred obligation.

If he succeeds, the entrepreneur becomes a "Business Owner." The fruits of success begin to come to him. Now he can afford to get involved in activities outside his business, to become established in social and civic concerns. He becomes active in his trade association, though usually years after the time when it could have really helped him.

You would think that now he would have less need for secrecy. Disaster is a distant possibility. What used to be called "kiting checks," becomes "working the float." (In publicly owned companies, it's called "cash management." It doesn't really matter what you call it, but, somehow, as the sums get bigger, it becomes more sophisticated and more prestigious to deal in checks that aren't any good when written.)

Things get going fast and furious. Now the business owner finds new reasons for secrecy. Once it hid how bad things were. Now he needs it either to cover up the "exorbitant" amount he's taking out of the business, or (and this is more common than most of us would like to think) to varnish over the fact that he's not *quite* as successful as his bluster would make it seem.

The business owner plays games with his accounting system because both Uncle Sam and his other greedy relatives seem to discourage blatant honesty. After all, there's the Florida branch office, the company Mercedes, the business meetings in Bermuda, a whole list of things that would be "misunderstood."

So the secrecy continues, and, because it continues, nobody yet knows enough either to question or to rationally support any of The Boss's judgements and business decisions. This lack of review may have been affordable when the business was being built on genius and sweat. Now, however, *the successful business needs more than talent and hard work. It needs management and planning for the future to keep it growing, profitable, and successful*.

But secrecy is to management and planning what frost is to avocados.

This is why so many successful business owners end their careers torn between the "divinity" of success and the terrors of loneliness, doubt, and fear. They are admired by everyone because of their success, but deep down in their hearts they keep asking themselves "What's right? What's fair? How come, if I'm so smart, I'm not sure I know what I'm doing?"

Advisors, consultants, and other sellers of services of all descriptions can earn their living forever feeding on the business owner's doubts and fears of "what if..." They never seem to go away.

By his secrecy, the entrepreneur is trapped into doing everything by himself, or trying to do it in collusive conjunction with a sequential series of individual "experts," who happen to share his bias. (And why shouldn't they? "Whatthehell," their thinking goes, "he's paying me for it. Best to give him what he wants and not bring up or pursue unpleasant subjects unless we're in agreement") But events begin to show him that his granite-like genius just can't handle the increasing load.

A sound, growing business in today's world is too complex for any one person to master all of its ramifications, no matter how capable that person is.

Sooner or later, every business owner needs real, honest, concerned help from people who are not self-serving. The sooner he realizes this and does something about it, the sooner he will be able to turn his talents back to making the business grow and meet the needs of the future.

The business owner needs a little bit of remedial training before he's ready to go out looking for outside directors, but he doesn't have the luxury of being able to "work on it." The older he gets, the tougher it's going to be for him to admit he needs help—and the tougher it gets to ask for it...or to give it to him.

In too many businesses, help is neither sought nor given. The purpose of the rest of this book is to help change all of that.

Chapter 2

Real Boards and What They Can Do

Business owners, their successors, their managers, and their families suffer from a very common problem: like lighthouse keepers and Himalayan monastics, they inhabit a *very* small world. The few times they do discuss business, it's mostly to or among themselves, and only about the business they inhabit. Outside of the very small world in which they live, their "facts" are mostly hearsay.

In most family companies, nearly all thinking and activity centers on immediate concerns, sudden problems, and petty disagreements. Value judgments, operating policies, and major assumptions are seldom recognized, rarely questioned, much less changed. They could safely be chiseled in marble above the office door—and stay there, unchanged, for decades.

At first, the important, wider questions are ignored because there just isn't enough time to think about them. Later, they're ignored because, well, we've always ignored "m—and look how well we've done.

This is the trend that has to be reversed if the family business is to survive , and this reversal has to start *inside* the business.

The family business, like any living, growing thing, needs a constant supply of sunshine and fresh air. It needs openings to the outside world. Instead, what tends to happen is the corporate shades are drawn lower and lower as the years go by, and issues which could have been solved by discussion become, in darkness and silence, serious and nagging problems.

If a business owner doesn't know how to share his problems and his hopes with his family, his managers, and his advisors, he has to learn. The business owner needs to develop ways he can share these problems and hopes with people whose opinions he accepts—and he will only accept opinions given out of respect or out of love. Both motives are acceptable.

But *he* has to do something. It's up to him to bring some of the really difficult—but crucial—questions into the open. In whatever form, communication and openness can be the beginning of a periodic, but increasingly regular review of *all* of the important questions about family business management and continuity.

The sooner the founder learns to share his problems and hopes, and the sooner he gets used to the cold shock of being questioned by outsiders, the sooner he will be ready to take that ultimate step of creating and installing a true business forum: a legally constituted body charged with ensuring the growth and continuity of the business—a working board of outside directors.

BOARDS WERE CREATED FOR A REASON

Boards of directors weren't just thrown in as baroque gingerbread on the corporate architecture. They weren't just bureaucratic dreams of hyperactive legislators. Boards of directors were placed in the corporate hierarchy with one simple objective: protecting the *continued* financial integrity of corporations. To this end, directors are held ultimately responsible for the management of the corporations they direct.

Note that the word is "management," not "managing." Directors are *directors*, not managers, and their responsibility is to the owners of the company, not the president.

This is true whether the company is publicly or privately held. The board is in a "fiduciary" relationship to the shareholders, which means that it is expected to act in their best interests. *It's in the definition of just what these "best interests" are that we find the difference between the duties of directors in private companies and directors in public companies* .

First we should consider how these duties are *similar* . These are the functions an *ideal* board in an *ideal* company should perform:

1) Helping the CEO set general objectives and major policies.

2) Helping the CEO fill board vacancies and electing corporate officers.

3) Helping the CEO select his successor.

4) Advising the CEO on important issues.

5) Judging the performance of the chief executive officer (CEO), rewarding or replacing as necessary.

That's the ideal. The facts of life, however, aren't all that crisp and clean. Real boards in public companies too often perform few of these functions. Real boards in family-owned businesses almost never do (after all, whose business is it, anyway?)

Generally, in a public company, the board is expected to protect the interests of the shareholders against inappropriate actions by management. But in the family-owned business, "protecting the shareholders' interests" often becomes a matter of protecting the business from both the actions and the inactions of the shareholder/managers themselves, as they respond to short-term or personal needs that may be in conflict with the long-term needs of the business.

It's one thing, for example, to have many thousands of shareholders, each unknown to the other, each interested only in return on investment. It's an entirely different matter to have very *few* shareholders, each with significant present or future ownership shares *and each with a voice in management* .

When shareholders are few and well known to each other, the result is too often a continuing reinvestment/dividend/ benefit battle. The temptation is great to pursue personal ambitions under the guise of business requirements, and even greater to ignore management responsibility because of the temptation to concentrate on matters of more personal importance.

The laws of our modern capitalistic society (wherein taxation has become a major instrument of governmental policy) have created chaos, where once there was at least the possibility of unified shareholder agreement. In too many "closely held" corporations, a controlling interest offers many ways for "creative" business expensing of disproportionate and varying benefits to managers and owners. The temptation of pre-tax incomes or benefits worth nearly double what they would be after-tax has clouded many "business" decisions.

The Internal Revenue Service and minority (unbenefitted) shareholders often find themselves strange bedfellows in their mutual attempts to limit what they consider the excessive (unfair/illegal) benefits enjoyed by those in power. Where the IRS and minority shareholders differ, however, is that the "deprived" shareholders will quickly drop *their* posture of righteous indignation if they are given a share of the spoils.

Needless to say, this constant bickering and concern over equal "entitlement" at the board level (where it usually occurs) effectively dilutes / confuses / eliminates any efforts to manage the business assets for the best interest of the company *as a whole*.

The director of a public corporation can safely place the interests of the whole corporation above the interests of any single shareholder or group of shareholders. That's usually the best way to ensure the best overall return on investment for the greatest number. There's an escape hatch, too. If a shareholder in a public company does not agree with the direction the board is going, the option available is a simple one. That shareholder can sell his shares on the open market to someone who does agree.

But in a family company, the director's job is not usually so straightforward. Shareholders in a family company cannot generally "vote" with their ownership. They cannot express their dissatisfaction by selling at will, because there is seldom any market for their shares. Owners of small blocks of stock tend to become thorns in the sides of owner-managers. There have even been books written on the techniques of oppressing and expelling minority shareholders.

Additionally, there is the whole subject of "valuation." What *is* the company worth—and to whom? What's it worth to majority owners, to minority owners, to investors, to the IRS? To a buyer it's one thing. To a seller, it's another.

In a closely held company, the interests of the company are often defined as equivalent to the interests of a few owners. Ownership and management get all enmeshed and confused. For tax reasons, "return on investment" takes on all sorts of exotic definitions, some of which may be good for the owners, but devastating for the business—or vice-versa.

In a family company, the economic interest of the company and the personal interests of the shareholders must be considered *together*, and they must be considered with common sense, compassion, wisdom, and understanding of what business ownership really means.

One of the greatest contributions a good board meeting can make to the well-being of a successful business owner is to offer him a time and place where—and peers with whom—he can feel challenged and comfortable, disciplined and secure, all at the same time. He can be reassured in the knowledge that their sole purpose is to be on his side, to help him make hard decisions, to help him resolve his uncertainties, to help him see clearly and act decisively under conditions of stress.

Harassment, turmoil, and mistrust have no place in any purposeful meeting of the board. Instead, directors must contribute direction, cooperation, and, ultimately, support. These are duties that arise from their desire to serve the owner-manager who seeks their help. And the business owner has nowhere else to look. This help is available only through an outside board.

WHY EVEN GOOD ADVISORS AREN'T ENOUGH

The business owner's managers and his advisors—his accountant, his banker, his attorney, agents, and consultants of all types—are paid, professional technicians. He needs them for his tactical planning and for facing the battles at hand. Too often, however, they become one sided technical advocates, unwilling to participate in the human considerations and consequences of contingent risk. "What if....?"

The advice of professional advisors needs to be supplemented by the thoughts of *strategists* , people whose concern is the total thrust of the business and where it is going.

The business owner constantly faces fundamental risk judgements, and his best source of overall help in making these judgements is a group of competent, experienced, *risk-taking peers* . What the founder and the business both need—in addition to competent technical advice—is the tested knowledge and experience of those who can be put in the position of being able to confirm or challenge the *risk* judgments of the owner—not just financial or legal judgements, but also emotional and familial judgements, with all of their consequences.

Paid advisers have knowledge, of course, but rarely are they in the position to start challenging the owner's judgments. They work for him, after all. Their livelihood depends on his funds, his good will, and his continued blessing. Besides, the nature of their expertise and experience doesn't usually include the trade-offs, consequences, and decisions of ownership. They are observers by nature, analyzers and recommenders by profession, and decision *makers* only by default.

It's one thing to give an owner-manager advice on, say, cash flow management or government regulation. It's an entirely different thing to understand and help a man whose personal and corprate goals are all intertwined, whose personal limits are often the limits he imposes on the company, and whose age increasingly becomes a factor in his decision making.

A risk-taking peer will have been through all that. He will understand. And he's not intimidated by the owner-manager's bluster and power.

Directors of a family-owned company, if they protect anybody, should protect the president from the dangers inherent in his own authority. Anyone who is going to act as a legitimate pressure group on an owner-manager must be someone who is capable of handling the founder's pride as well as of withstanding his onslaughts.

Over and above the obvious (though most often neglected) areas of technical, financial, organizational, and managerial direction and review, directors of a family business *must* also be able to deal with such issues as:

> *What are the true needs for the future? For the business? For the family?*
>
> *Who should share the burdens and risks, and how?*

How much growth/change is necessary/ helpful/indispensible to stability and progress in the future?

What effects will this have on the organization, present and future?

What are the varying and unique considerations in each transition of ownership and management that will affect the people involved (both active and inactive owners, as well as family and non-family managers)?

Which, if any, of the available heirs can/ should be the primary leader in the future?

What about a non-family manager as CEO?

Who will determine the qualities and abilities of the potential successors? Mother? Dad? Who really knows them?

Must heirs be successors?

Do job rights go with all stock inheritance?

What is "fair"?

How can accommodation/acceptance in the family be assured?

How can both family and managerial pressures be given appropriate attention?

When should transition occur? What are its ramifications for management? For retirement?

...to name only a few.

These questions must be answered. They won't disappear because we avoid the subject, and our natural reluctance to confront the *inevitability* of the future only makes the problem worse. Emotions heighten. Time becomes limited. Positions harden. If ever there was a need to plan ahead and then act on those plans, it's in the affairs of a family in business.

This is the primary area where a board of risk-taking peers can serve, and it can serve in many ways. It can help the business owner as a profit maker, by adding to the overall expertise of the company. Both in the long run as well as the short run, it can act as a governor or safety switch, protecting both the CEO and his business from unconscious overloads on both, and it can act as a surrogate authority, when and as necessary. Ultimately, in its responsibility for continuity of the enterprise, a board can be a judgemental body, watching, evaluating, and helping choose among alternative potential successors and succession plans.

The aid of outside directors is absolutely necessary if the one man show the founder has built is going to be successfully perpetuated into the next generation. The outside director must help answer the important questions *in ways acceptable to everyone involved*. And there are many people involved: owners (single or multiple) and their families, managers and their concerns, employees and their security—plus customers, suppliers, and the community, all of whom have an interest in its success.

To do this, a board must apply itself to a whole range of activities.

DIRECTORS AS "PLANNERS"

A working board of outside directors can provide the owner-manager with a vehicle for doing the *strategic planning* he must do. It can help him set goals, define objectives, decide where he's going, determine the risk involved, and estimate the rewards that are possible.

Owner-managers too often tend to confuse strategy with tactics—and the loser, almost automatically, is strategy. Tactical planning, generally, isn't The Boss's job. The management team exists to carry out, tactically, whatever strategic decisions have been made on a higher level. This assumes, of course, a higher level exists.

As a company grows in size and complexity, the need for strategic attention becomes even more important. This is why a board becomes increasingly necessary with success, and why the typical decisions made by working boards are long-range and policy in nature.

For examples, boards typically approve:

* *Annual capital and operating budgets .*
* *Product addition and deletion decisions .*
* *Acquisition or merger considerations .*
* *Selection, development, responsibility, and compensation of key managers.*
* *Major price changes .*
* *Long-term contractual agreements .*
* *Major financial commitments*
* *Building plans .*

...and other such actions which have significant impact on the future of the company. In family companies, there are also the ever-present concerns of the owner(s), concerns the directors must also address:

* *Where are we going?*
* *Who is going to be responsible?*
* *Who/what are we doing all this for, anyway?*

For successful business owners, financial success is only the beginning. Solving the problems of survival never solves all the problems—new pressures and concerns come with success and they're as demanding and complex as those the founder fought in the beginning. He wonders, for example, why he is working harder now than he ever did. He's worried that the business he's built with such care will crumble because he is the only person who can run it. He's concerned that his spouse and his children don't really understand his hopes and dreams for the future.

Solutions to each of these, and other, questions usually require significant changes of direction. They require strategic decisions. The nuts and bolts of carrying out these decisions are, themselves, complicated and delicate matters, but are properly the province of the key managers and advisors.

Strategy and tactics are best considered as separate responsibilities, primarily because of the tendency tactical concerns have to narrow perspective. It's okay for a lieutenant to concentrate on taking Hill X, but if the colonel or the general get involved with decisions on that level, the entire army would eventually forget the reason Hill X was important in the first place. Where do they go from there?

DIRECTORS AS "SAFETY FUSES"

Omnipotence is really not all it's cracked up to be—at least not for us mortals—and many, if not most, of the successful owner-manager's problems are caused by the very fact of his almost absolute power. Both he and the business need protection.

The threats, in this sense, don't come from outside the business. There are plenty of external dangers, of course, but a specific area where a board can help is protection from the *internal* dangers.

Originally, a board can protect the new CEO from his fantasies and his overaggressiveness. Dreams are like girl friends. They can be fun to have around, even beneficial, but real love and a true future are built on a spouse. For the CEO, the "spouse" is performance, the *accomplished* dream, and to perform, he must turn his dreams into practical plans. A good board can push him to do this. We've all had the experience of pursuing fantasies, but eventually we learn that it's what gets *done*, not what we *dream* about that counts. So we learn to work hard at what we do.

But even successful owner-managers don't stay young forever. Slowly, steadily, age becomes an increasingly influential partner in the business owner's life, and the board's protection role changes over time. Where it previously protected him against over-aggressive pursuit of fantasy, *it will inevitably find itself more and more in the role of balancing a growing conservatism* .

"If I could only keep what I have!" the business owner finds himself muttering in the middle of the night. Growth means more hard work, more risk. Increasingly, the owner-manager has had enough of that. His outside directors can serve to remind him that growth is essential, while helping him minimize both the necessary risk and the energy demands.

DIRECTORS AS "SUPPORTERS"

The family business faces some considerable dangers, too, most of them no different from dangers public companies face. In the case of the family company, however, the importance of these threats can be so much greater, because their impact can be so much more devastating.

Lack of Market Intelligence. There is an unceasing need for information, for understanding of the marketplace. What is happening in other industries? What is the collective judgement on the state, and future, of the economy? Directors represent, each in their own way, new circles of market understanding and intelligence.

A board can provide a business owner with some very valuable—and necessary—creative input. Objective outside directors can bring to the company a non-involved viewpoint. They can be relatively free of concern for the effect their ideas have on immediate operations (new ideas, after all, always mean more work and more problems for somebody).

Directors can, in fact, provide a valuable *combination* of biased viewpoints, filtering operating intelligence through unique perspectives. Objectivity, true objectivity, is not really possible—and, it's not necessarily creative. We see what we are prepared to see, so it is a good thing to have other people's biased views.

Capable outside directors, therefore, will challenge the inevitable assumptions and sacred cows within existing management policy. Because of their different circles and experience, they can also be a way to expand the founder's existing circle of competent professional advisors, and increase the contact a business owner has with potential management personnel.

Over-Betting. There is a vast gulf between true budget-making and business fantasy, but that gulf is often not obvious to the fantasizer. It's amazing the kind of salutory effect such simple questions as, "Do you really think you're going to be able to...?" or "What happens if you don't...?" can have on the planning process. And a good board can take this one step further by adding, "Here's why we do/don't think you should..."

Under-Management. We all think our businesses are different, but a board can and should force the business owner to put into effect the many tried and tested controls, measures, and procedures that can apply to every business. Left to himself, the owner-manager would most likely see these techniques as useless brakes on his "creative genius."

Poor or Unaggressive Advisors. Advisors are a seemingly unending problem for business owners, who seldom seem satisfied with their attorneys, their accountants, their bankers, you name 'm. "If I knew good advice when I saw it," the frustrated owner-manager will say, "I wouldn't need it—I'd provide it myself." Well, because of wider (collective) experience, a board can do a very effective "compared-to-what-and-whom" analysis on existing advice and advisors, helping the business owner determine whether or not he has the best available.

Tragedy. The unspeakable can happen, even to us. If a CEO is a one-man show (as he almost invariably is), there's often no other drummer to which the business can march. If The Boss falls out of the parade, there's no more parade. Against this eventuality, a good, working board is one of the best protections around. Almost from the beginning, a board can work to help recast the one-man band into a smoothly running organization.

In the event the untimely happens, that board can help provide the necessary management continuity to help make sure the business adapts and continues. It can also help provide the time needed to make the necessary adjustments.

If ever we need comfort and support, it's after the death of a spouse. Since there's enough sorrow and trauma accompanying such events, a widow doesn't need more problems. Instead, she needs the comfort that comes from knowledge that solutions to the *economic* problems of the business are in good hands and that she can feel secure in the help of those responsible for its (and her) well being. A working board of objective outsiders can be a great comfort here.

DIRECTORS AS "BIG BROTHERS"

Sooner or later, the successful business owner begins to think of himself as "divine." This is one of the dubious fruits of success. *He* did it, after all, and because *He* did, He begins to confuse some very crucial virtues:

He confuses omnipotence ("It's MY business") with omniscience ("I KNOW what's best for the company") .

This must be true, he reasons, because he made all the decisions over the years, and it did all work out. Nobody else even made a suggestion. It's only natural for The Boss to assume the "dummies" kept their mouths shut because they didn't know what to say, especially in the face of his continuing managerial brilliance.

He confuses success ("What I built...") with ability ("... with my genius") .

Over the years, it becomes almost impossible for the successful business owner to look with anything but personal pride at the business that's grown out of the shop he started in his garage. He remembers very well the early years. He remembers the anxiety and the doubts. He asks himself: Who else could have survived all that other than a genuine genius? Don't try to tell a business owner about luck, or favorable economic conditions, or the power of being in the right place at the right time. He won't listen to any of that because he knows better.

He built a successful business, and to him this means much more than being the best at what he does best. To him, it means he's the best at *everything* he does.

He confuses obesience ("Yassuh, Boss") with agreement ("Good idea, Boss") .

The successful business owner, in his world, is an absolute monarch. All the marbles are his, and he knows very well how to rattle those marbles. Naturally everybody agrees with him. They know if they don't they'll be out on the street. Sheer discretion dictates that the business owner's courtiers defer readily and completely to his ideas.

We know of some small towns where people are actually tempted to take their hats off when they talk to the business owner on the phone. He knows it. He loves it. Success leads to power, to respect, to deference, and to dependence.

Well, after a few years of this, the business owner, himself, (who should know better—and once did) begins to believe all this adulation.

Almost inevitably, the successful business owner falls victim to the byproducts of personal success. He confuses applause with respect. He confuses experience with understanding. He confuses his ever-expanding influence with immortality. He even confuses his wishes with reality.

But none of these are equivalent, and a good board will tell him so—as often and as forcefully as necessary.

WHY DIRECTORS AND SUCCESSORS SHOULD BE FRIENDS

A working board can act as a "court of appeals" for successors, in spite of the fact that those successor-managers sometimes see outside directors as just another of Dad's tactics to make doubly sure he gets his way.

It may be true that Dad is only using the board as a tactic, but even his questionable motives won't alter a major truth: a working board can be as much the succesor-manager's support as the owner-manager's.

In any family company with an outside board, there's going to come that important day when the directors are presented with a fundamental disagreement between The Boss and his successor(s). When that happens, there's usually a long moment of heavy silence. It's a crucial moment, and everybody in the room realizes it. A fundamental question is being addressed.

Whatever the specific disagreement might be is not as important as what it represents, because down deep the real issue is almost always the same thing—finding agreement on directions for the future.

Just for example, let's say the subject at issue is expansion into a new product line, and the proponent of the expansion is (who else?) a successor.

He's given the board all his numbers. He's done his homework. The potential rewards (very high), as well as the risks (also very high) are stated. He thinks the future of the company depends upon this kind of expansion and he says so. He's adamant that the risk *must* be taken.

The Boss, on the other hand, is convinced the risk is too great. He explains that he tried expansions like this himself in the past and they failed. He also points out that his entire net worth is tied up in the present company, which is profitable. He believes it's foolish to risk so much on a questionable new venture, and doesn't hestitate to say so—emphatically.

The meeting isn't the first time this disagreement has come up—it's just the culmination of a long and seemingly fruitless "discussion" between The Boss and his successor(s).

Here is where we can begin to see the true value of a board of outside directors to the business, to the owner-manager—and to the successors.

The question to be answered—whatever the specifics of the disagreement—is how to move aggressively into the future without destroying the value and security that's been built in the past.

The board has to help answer this question if it's going to fulfil its responsibility to the company. But—and this is important for successors to understand—to do that, the board must protect the interests of *both* the owner-manager and the successors.

What each wants for the company has value. Though they appear to represent opposing views, usually they really represent opposite poles of a single truth.

The founder has a legitimate interest in his *security*, which usually is tied intimately into the security of the company. So his concern is as much for the stability of the business as it is for his own future.

Many once successful family businesses have been destroyed through unwise expansion or investment. A good working board will put a lot of effort into avoiding this pitfall by subjecting any new venture to some really tough scrutiny.

But the board is also charged with the responsibility for *continuity*. That's the Boss's dream, too. After all, that should be a major reason why he created and installed the outside board in the first place.

The future is mostly the *successors'* business, though, and here is where the board will be working in the successors' interest, doing some very important favors for them in the process.

First, whether or not it sides with the successors on a particular issue, the board of directors is going to force the company to make long range plans .

Since a successor-management is going to be managing the company in the future, the sooner that future is defined and work starts on making it happen, the sooner the successors will know there *is* a future, and that somebody besides the successors believes in it.

Another benefit tied into this long range planning—and one the successors might not recognize right away—is that early planning takes advantage of the true genius and experience of the present owner-manager. The chance to plan while Dad is still around to cooperate can be a major blessing.

Secondly, the board is going to see that a succession plan is put in place .

This means that the successor-managers must be designated—even if tentatively. They must also be able to carry out whatever long-range plans have been set, so they have to be trained.

Formal training is not usually given a high priority in family businesses. It's not likely that Dad ever had any, so usually there's "no time" for something he doesn't respect or understand. But it has to be done, and the board will see that it is. Without this preparation, chances are good the successor-management won't be qualified to take advantage of tomorrow's opportunities.

A succession plan also means a timetable must be set up for the transfer of responsibility to the successors. This isn't a technique for getting rid of the Old Man. It's a discipline on his successors to perform to expectations, and to deliver that performance on time.

Finally, the board is going to defuse and arbitrate potential disagreements —both business and personal—and this takes us back to the example cited earlier.

That situation illustrates how important a *mutually respected forum* can be. This isn't to say that the board is going to side with the successors—or The Boss. The point is that extremes aren't the only answers. If a compromise is possible (and best) the board will lead the way. When Boss and successors meet toe to toe, they need outside help to keep from bloodying their respective noses.

The board doesn't only work between successors and The Boss, however. Working as a manager for "the divinity" is no picnic, either. Who, for example, is going to judge the competence and performance of those managers whose style and opinions differ greatly from The Boss's? Who's going to choose key managers from among competing managers, while maintaining an aura of objectivity? Who is going to judge? Can The Boss do this from his head rather than his gut? He needs—and knows he needs—help.

WHY INSIDERS NEED OUTSIDERS

Objections to installing outsiders on family business boards are continually strong and recurring. Most business owners have very definite reasons for resisting the notion. Too often they look upon any "board of directors" as a damn nuisance, required by law as a sort of trade off for gaining the corporate status which provides: (a) limited liability, (b) preferential tax treatment ("loopholes" to those without them), or (c) the ability to raise capital from others (how else can you sell stock to your brother-in-law?). Seldom do they see their boards serving the purpose for which boards were originally created—to provide a vehicle for ensuring the continiuty of a "legal person." So they prostitute the idea by filling the required positions with shills.

Every corporation has a set of bylaws, and in those bylaws various functions are assigned to the board. But in a privately owned business the powers assigned are too often left solely to The Boss, totally ignored, or, sometimes, deliberately flaunted. Too many directors do little more than sign the various papers the company's advisors draw up—without even reading them. After all, they say, it's The Boss's business.

No wonder, over the years, that business owners become convinced that a board of directors is one of the stupidest ideas ever invented by man. It's okay for the big corporations, but an unreasonable—and expensive, and unnecessary—burden for *his* company.

But, in the face of all the potential benefits of an outside board described above, the assumed advantages of an inside board should begin to pale. It's true that insiders are much better informed about the business. It's true that insiders probably know the industry from top to bottom. It's true that insiders understand very well how the company is organized and how the internal "politics" operate. But this knowledge and experience is already available to the company. We don't need to create board seats to take advantage of them. That's doing little more than rearranging the actors like we were running a repertory theater, where everybody plays every role, using the same limited talent.

So what is an outside board supposed to do? It's responsibilities are many, and they change as the business grows.

In the beginning, in the "survival years," a company can get along without a formal board. Boards exist in most start up corporations only because they are required by law. The surely don't have any real function. Most of the available energy is absorbed just keeping the doors open. Outsiders would just clutter up an already chaotic situation.

But once a business has survived and starts growing at some reasonably steady pace, the requirements for outside advice and review of the business owner and his plans (or lack of them) begin to increase. In the middle years, the years of growth, many critical decisions are made as to markets, products, personnel, and ownership distribution, and these decisions should be made under the scrutiny of competent, committed, contributory outsiders.

As even more time passes, the "trustee" role of the board becomes more and more important. All we have to do as successful business owners is ask ourselves what would happen today if we had our "heart attack." Or—and this is probably more important and increasingly pressing as we age—how can we arrange things so we can enjoy the fruits of a lifetime of labor? (We surely don't plan on dying, but we do start spending more and more time thinking about "letting go," "semi-retiring," "stepping down," or whatever terms we have for *taking it easier*.) If we don't like the answer or, worse, if we don't have the answer, we come across a vast hole in our planning, one that an outside board would have forced us to fill in long ago.

In the absence of any definitive answer, the typical business owner/founder either (a) works like a dog until he drops, (b) lets the business run down and lives off the assets in a drawn out liquidation, (in these cases, when he dies he leaves the problem to his widow and a mixed bag of Rasputins to solve, usually disastrously), or (c) sells out to somebody else and blames his decision on taxes, competitors, or the irresponsibility of the young.

Whichever route is chosen, another fine business disappears, and all the dreams of the founder(s) go with it.

Assuring the survival of a successful business is a great responsibility, one that becomes heavier and heavier as the company grows. After a certain point, it's a responsibility that's far beyond the capacity of the successful business owner to handle by himself.

This is the board's job. It's up to The Boss to make sure the right board exists to do that job.

Chapter 3

So How Do We Tell We Need One?

Not everyone needs an outside board .

In the early years, most owner-managed businesses get along just fine without ouside directors. In fact, most business founders would probably agree that, in those "interesting" days, outsiders would've just gummed up the works, tripped up decision making, and generally slowed things down.

Few start-up entrepreneurs have a need for anything other than cash, customers, energy, and more cash. Whatever brains might be needed are supplied by The Boss.

Besides, in the early years problems don't break down very readily into "shareholder" problems, or "board" problems, or "management" problems. To the business founder, problems are problems, usually big ones. If they're not solved on the spot—by whatever measures are available—there won't be any "later" to worry about. In reality, there are often many other more pressing and important requirements that must be fulfilled before the need for a board becomes important.

For the founder, the basic—and most important—requirement is survival. There are others, but this is the one that cracks him in the nose every morning at three a.m., as he lies awake, mulling over his dubious future.

But this pressing concern presses less as success arrives. Usually, his business changes faster than he realizes. The founder often doesn't notice, but as his business grows, his management style begins to change. He brings in more employees, more managers, sometimes even better advisors—certainly more expensive. His car gets classier. His office gets paneled. His tax bracket becomes permanent.

His business changes, too. It becomes more complicated—even petty cash becomes a controlled account. Markets enlarge. Customers become more diverse. The product line widens. To take care of all this, The Boss reacts, responds, and reorganizes as he goes.

He reorganizes, that is, everything except his "pseudo-board." No reason to change that, he figures.

He finds himself having more frequent conversations with advisors of all sorts—usually with conflicting opinions. He begins to talk more with other businessmen about business problems, comparing notes, sharing opinions, trading successes. (Most of these war stories are hearsay or fabrication, however—who wants to admit to the really stupid mistakes?). For the founder who's beginning to make it, the subject of how others face and solve problems becomes more and more fascinating.

He goes to conferences on every imaginable subject, and experts from out of town, whom he meets at exotic convention watering holes, begin to take on special appeal. He now "auditions" the advice he gets in his *ad hoc* search for "new ideas," making sure it agrees with his own opinion. If it doesn't agree with his existing assumptions, it's not a new idea, only a dumb idea from somebody who obviously "doesn't understand."

Things keep getting complicated, and the founder begins to lose that comfortable feeling he had about his ability to handle everything. As time passes, *this* is what keeps him up nights, although you can bet he won't admit it, even to himself.

We met a business owner at a seminar a few years back who had never really given the subject of an outside board of peers much thought. One night he was comparing notes with another participant, who happened to be a director in a company in another industry. It turned out that this other company had a much different employee-to-sales ratio, and they spent considerable time analyzing other respective ratios, asking each other penetrating questions.

As he said to us: "Then it hit me—here was a relative stranger who, by merely comparing notes with me, could be responsible for identifying problems in our company which I probably wouldn't have noticed. That was enough evidence for me that I needed people like him helping me."

This founder suddenly realized that honest discussion with outsiders was more beneficial in helping him run his business than he, himself, ever had the time, experience, or even the inclination to realize. For a long time, these kinds of questions hadn't seemed important enough for him to worry about. Suddenly, though, he realized his business was no longer the little shop he'd founded.

EXAMPLE OF A COMPANY IN NEED

Every successful family-owned business, left to itself, eventually reaches a point where the problems seem to outstrip the available solutions. This is an almost sure sign that the company is ready for a real board, and, too often, it's also a sign that The Boss waited too long to consider the idea of its creation. This doesn't often mean it's too late—just long overdue.

For example, we were recently involved in setting up an outside board for an industrial distribution business in the Midwest, a $20 million business with two 59-year-old owner-managers and a second generation of 25 to 30-year-old sons/successors, all working in the business.

Bill, 59, was CEO and 68% shareholder, and Al, also 59, was the executive vice president and 32% owner. Along with two other non-shareholding vice presidents in their 60's, they had worked together like brothers since the early 1950's to build their company.

Their situation was painfully typical. The need for professional managers to manage the company during the interim while the successors were being groomed was obvious to everyone but the management. They had been so busy running the business and believing they were immortal that it took a bomb to knock them into their last chance at reality.

Prior to the creation of its working outside board, the company directors were Bill, Al, and the company's attorney. What had persuaded them to seek help was the cancer surgery, two weeks before, on Mike, their vice president of sales. Mike was recovering from the successful operation, but his convalescence was expected to be at least three months long.

Bill wasn't worried as much about having Mike out for three months as he was about the sudden realization that the four "hotshots," as he put it, who started the business would all be past 60 in less than a year and there was nobody behind them. How, he wondered, did that happen?

It happened because problems like these always come on slowly, like failing eyesight or deafness. They happen so gradually that we don't notice them until some day we bump into a tree or walk into a wailing ambulance. At least Bill was luckier than some—he had enough time to get fitted out with business glasses and a hearing aid.

The company, as mentioned, had no outside directors. That was on the agenda for "someday" like so many other things. Now, suddenly, events had made the need obvious. The company was going to have to find and install a "missing generation" of managers, and a sound, functioning board was absolutely essential as a bridge.

Eventually, three outside directors were added to the company's board of directors. All were top people who complemented each other well. One was a 50-year-old, second generation owner of a very successful concrete products firm with national distribution. Another was the young former owner of a $12 million company, who'd merged with a public corporation and had stayed on to run the company. The third outsider was the professional manager of a $100 million construction equipment division of a diversified manufacturing company in an unrelated industry.

They were an excellent collection of talent, flattered to be asked, and eager to go to work on the new board which consisted of these three outsiders, plus Al and Bill. (The corporate attorney was glad to step down from the board and function solely as general counsel where he felt more comfortable. He'd wanted to do that for a long time, but was concerned that his "resignation" would be misinterpreted as a lack of support.)

WHERE A BOARD CAN...AND CANNOT...HELP

This new board decided at its first meeting that it had five major, high-priority objectives (each of them good examples of the kinds of needs best filled by a working board with a majority of outside directors).

First, they were going to have to be willing to accept, understand, and improve, if possible, Bill's and Al's estate plans.

The new directors realized that the death of either of the owners would mean a major change in their responsibilities.

While Bill and Al were around—which everyone hoped would be for a good, long time—their proper allegiance was to them as a *team* . But this, they understood, wouldn't always be the case. They had to ask themselves what the owners' plans would mean to them as directors and to the company, and how the board should react to those plans.

Each of the estate plans, as they were drawn when the new directors first took their seats, named as executors a tax accountant, the owners' wives, and a third party to be jointly chosen by the others. The question for the board: what would this plan mean to the company, and how could they implement it? While it was *not* for them to make judgements as to how, or to whom, the owners chose to distribute their assets, these actions would have far reaching consequences for the company. They knew they had to address this question.

Secondly, the board faced a generation of young inheritors who were just beginning to learn what they needed to know to run the business 10 or 15 years down the road.

The proper training of those young people was going to be crucial to guaranteeing the perpetuation of the company, and, therefore, had to become one of the prime responsibilities of the board.

In this particular family business, there were two shareholder families. Neither the children nor the parents of that upcoming generation were likely to have expectations and standards similar to those of professional management or of an outside board. Again, protection and continuity of the company was paramount while these varying viewpoints were reconciled.

Third, a professional interim management had to be selected.

The company, like so many others, had a need for more management talent than the owning families had, or could possibly have bred. This was going to be more than a simple recruitment problem, because the board would have to come to grips with some major questions. Why should, and how can non-family managers serve a privately owned business? What inducements and security would they need? What prudently could/should be offered to them? What should be their relationship to the upcoming successors?

Fourth, the company had to be reorganized to accommodate the new team.

Like most first-generation family companies, this company was designed *ad hoc.* What organization there was had been built up around the particular strengths and weaknesses of the present managers. This worked well for them, but would be useless, if not detrimental, to the outside managers the company was about to bring in. A major reorganization of jobs and responsibilities would surely become necessary very soon.

Fifth, a plan had to be made for the future of the present owners/key managers.

If a new team of young, aggressive managers was going to be installed, room had to be made for it, consistent with the needs, desires, and competence of the present managers who built the company. And all of this had to be managed in a way compatible with the future requirements of the company—and with *both* generations involved in the transition.

Like most important problems in family-owned businesses, these were complex matters that couldn't be solved overnight. But this new working board was just the body that could do something about it—and it did. The company's impressive turnaround over the last few years into a dynamic, aggressive, future-oriented business is proof of their contribution.

THE SIGNALS THAT INDICATE A BOARD IS NECESSARY

One good way to look at the question of "when is a board needed?" is to look at what a board is supposed to do. If the *functions* a board normally provides are needed by a company, then a board is probably needed.

The traditional responsibilities of boards are usually broken down into five broad categories:

a) *Review and authorization of both corporate and financial strategy* ,

b) *Establishment of policies and plans to implement those strategies* ,

c) *Formation and maintainence of the management team* ,

d) *Creation of good corporate controls* , and

e) *Review and approval of employee and community relations* .

Look at each of these responsibilities in turn, then examine your family company to see if these needs are there. If so, there's good reason to believe that the advice and influence of outside directors is needed, and that maybe Mother and Uncle Virgil just aren't up to doing the job.

A) Corporate and Financial Strategy.

The board is usually expected to oversee major corporate and financial decisions and is the ultimate source of approval for any changes in capital structure. For example, the board is usually the authority for any change in company securities, and how they are issued, transferred, and registered.

Major financial decisions are also usually under the supervision of the board. Boards generally approve any decisions made about dividend distribution, for example. No major company assets can be disposed of without board approval, nor can long-term debt or major short-term loans be taken out without board approval.

If a family-owned company finds itself getting into situations where major financial commitments are required, or major changes in asset structure and/or capitalization are contemplated, the advice and input of outside directors is probably needed, and creation of a board should be seriously considered. It's truly amazing how the requirement to explain our needs and actions to "outsiders" helps clarify our thinking— for *our* benefit!

B) Policy Making.

The need for formalizing policy indicates that a company is moving beyond the day-to-day survival stage, and that the owners are beginning to lift their noses from the grindstone long enough to consider the future seriously.

In this context, boards are typically asked to approve the annual capital and operating budgets which are so essential to the whole planning process. It's the businessman's equivalent of the professional pilot's need to have a flight plan approved *before* he takes off. They can also get involved in such important questions as whether or not a new line of business (or dropping an old line) is a good idea. Boards should approve acquisitions and mergers, major price policies, long-term contractual agreements, major organizational restructuring, building plans—or any other decisions which involve such significant changes of direction or emphasis within a company that management needs or wants to have a review of its thinking— *before* acting on it.

These are *strategy* decisions. This is how a company decides it is going to fight the war. The job of management is to carry out strategy, to make the day-to-day, *tactical* decisions needed to win the battles that are fought in support of that major strategy. The reason a board is responsible for strategy or policy is that management tends—for very good reason—to have its mind in the field. As one fellow said, "When you're up to your butt in crocodiles, it's kinda hard to remember your job was to drain the swamp."

The *long-range* point of view is often best concentrated in the heads of those who don't also have to fight the everyday battles.

As an owner-manager finds his business growing and succeeding, he finds himself more and more involved with strategic questions. In the beginning, as we said before, survival is the key word. Survival is a *tactical* question. But, later, growth, and its definition, become major concerns, and the problems of growth are often as much strategic in nature as they are tactical.

As time goes by, strategic questions begin to dominate the president's job, and when strategy decisions start to arise with increasing frequency and impact, a business is ready for an outside board.

C) Forming and Maintaining the Management Team.

Boards of directors usually have broad responsibility and authority over key managers that arise directly out of their responsibility to ensure the continuity of the business. Boards typically define the duties of the chief executive officer (CEO), approve the appointment of corporate officers, appraise the performance of the key managers (usually as a team, but often individually), and approve compensation plans, including that of the CEO.

The board is also usually responsible for defining or approving overall directions and objectives of management development programs. Proper training of future key managers is important for corporate survival.

Even more important, though, is the board's responsibility to provide for an orderly succession in the president/CEO chair. Succession takes on an even wider significance in the closely held company than it has in the public corporation, because, in the family company, succession to the job of president usually implies some form of ownership transition, and, as such, doesn't usually happen more than once every generation.

A business founder can usually see when his company is reaching the point where the recruiting and development of a management team is becoming important to success. This is the time, usually, when the "old guard" is doing an adequate job, but doesn't seem up to the demands and pace of the future. This is also a point at which the owner-founder finds that his presence is indispensible to the company.

It may be flattering, but, given the fact that we are all mortal, The Boss's indispensibility is an intolerable situation for any company planning on a chance at continuity.

In this kind of situation, a board is usually the best vehicle for change—it doesn't necessarily share The Boss's assumptions, and it can often see a new need where he can only see a reaffirmation of his own genius and talent. It's hard to be humble when you're so damn good!

D) Corporate Controls.

Closely tied to questions of policy are questions of whether the policies already in place are working. Measuring performance on this scale is a matter of control. Boards are typically charged with the responsibility for reviewing company performance, which requires that there be a system that supplies the necessary information to the directors.

As performance is examined, boards are expected to look into problems, identify areas where management is deficient, and propose ways to correct unsatisfactory situations. Clearly, this is a responsibility that management cannot effectively perform, because that would involve judging its own performance.

E) Employee and Community Relations.

There are a number of decisions about corporate employees which can have strategic significance, and these are usually best left to the board of directors. Among these questions are the type and extent of benefit plans, contractual decisions affecting the unions, hiring and firing practices, and compliance with a whole host of governmentally mandated personnel policies (whether we agree with them or not).

While such employee questions may be more common and pressing in the larger, public corporations, as closely held businesses grow and expand in employment, personnel decisions can begin to have a major impact on performance.

When an owner-manager finds that the interests of the company and the expressed interests of the employees are starting to diverge in a very significant way, he is ready for the help and advice of risk-taking peers, preferably people who have already faced these questions.

As to a corporation's community obligations, few founders or inheritors have the sensitivity or the courage to appreciate what our modern society is increasingly expecting from its corporate citizens. Determining a company's proper response to these new pressures and opportunities is a challenge to the best of boards.

HOW TO KNOW WHEN YOU'RE READY

At what point does an owner-manager need this outside help...and review? Well, if you ask him, all other things being equal he will probably say "never." But the truth is that all of us, at all times, need some form of helpful review. That goes for artists as well as it does for businessmen. It is true for everyone. Review is discipline. Review is guidance. Review is a refreshment of thoughts and ideas. For the purpose of review alone, the creation of an outside board is worth consideration.

Even the brand new entrepreneur could use some form of dispassionate review to make sure he's not unwittingly cutting his own throat. But he rarely asks for it—and even more rarely accepts it.

Some rules of thumb might be helpful. Since the primary function of an outside board in a family company is to ensure profitable growth, continuity, and a smooth ownership-management transition with succession, a family company must generally meet the following conditions before it is ready for a board:

1) **The company should be successful.** This doesn't mean the company must be vastly profitable, nor even that it must be currently profitable. What it does mean is that a company is only ready for an outside board once it is an established, going concern

with reasonable expectations of making it in the future.

The start-up business has one primary objective—survival. There is usually no time, no energy, nor even any willingness to listen to the suggestions and ideas of outsiders. Survival problems are immediate problems, problems of tactics rather than strategy, *and a board of directors is not generally designed to deal with tactics* .

Survival is not a problem confined only to start up businesses, however. Sometimes going concerns find themselves in serious trouble due to changes in management, markets, competition, productivity, and so forth. This, too, is a survival problem. "Successful" should also be interpreted to mean a reasonable probability that any unfortunate present situation is only temporary, and that there are sound long term prospects for survival and profitable growth.

Boards should *not* be created to perform crisis surgery.

2) **There should be some reasonably stable management structure.** This means defined duties and divided responsibilities. Without such a structure, there is really no business entity which can experience "continuity," and a working board would be superfluous. What this kind of company needs is management, not directors.

Structure does not imply size, however. Family-owned companies with two key managers can have as valid a need for a formal outside board as companies with 20 managers. Structure merely guarantees that the managers are working in some organized and directed way, and that the directors will have some organization to direct.

Another way to state this requirement would be to say that every company reaches a point at which it becomes important to separate owning from managing. This separation doesn't have to be done in fact. We're certainly not recommending that owners avoid involvement with the management of their own companies. However, it does mean that every successful business owner has to be able, somehow, to separate the responsibilities, benefits, and authority that accrue to him as the owner, from the responsibilities, benefits, and authority he has as manager. This is particularly important in businesses with multiple ownership.

It's common in family businesses to have two or more owners who have equal shares in the business. Often this happens because businesses started out as partnerships and later incorporated. Sometimes a founder has to bring in silent (or not-so-silent) partners because of particular cash or management needs. Second generation businesses almost always end up with multiple owners as the founder divides his 100% among his heirs and other "beneficiaries." Whatever the objective of setting up these "committees" of ownership, they often wind up mired in very sticky confusions between *shareholder* rights and *management* rights.

A 50-50 ownership split, say, does nothing to alter the primary organizational fact of life that there can only be one CEO. In a new business, such structural questions are just little seedlings in the jungle called survival. Partners can operate a startup business very efficiently because *doing* is more important than *structure* . Eventually, though, structure becomes as important as action. In fact, without structure, action will, at some point, become impossible.

When a company is reaching the point where the unspoken and undefined structure everybody has taken for granted can no longer be taken for granted, it is reaching the point where it needs a formal working board. If for no other reason, the board will be needed to help define the management needs and how they differ from the ownership needs—as well as to establish a priority of opinion.

3) **The managers and advisors should be as competent and well-chosen as possible.** There is little a board can do to help management with its planning if there is nobody capable of having good ideas—or of making good suggestions—in the first place. Directors are neither replacements for incompetant legal

or financial advisors, nor substitutes for irresponsible, undeveloped, or unqualified managers.

A working board is the final polish put on a well-designed and functioning structure. The business must have the required talent and ability among its managers and advisors to be able to provide needed information to the board in an organized and intelligent way. Those same people must then be able to explain or defend decisions and actions to the board. Conversely, these managers must also be able to translate the policy decisions made by the board into action.

Without such a management team, a working board is as ineffective as a conductor without an orchestra.

Once the board is installed and functioning, one of its major responsibilities will be to ensure that this strong and effective management team has not only top level support, but also the depth required for continuity. As businesses grow through one management transition to another, it usually becomes more and more necessary to recruit the necessary management talent from outside the owning families. That is not a job families do naturally—nepotisim having the attractive glitter that it does—and the responsibility often falls on the shoulders of the outside directors to balance the needs of the company with the natural tendency toward nepotism.

Let us state here, however, that nepotism should not be regarded as equivalent to incest. In most cases, family businesses continue *only* because of the existance of qualified, motivated, risk-taking, and annointed family successors. But blood (or marriage) *alone* does not a manager make. Some nepots would do themselves and their companies untold good by staying out, entirely. A family business is not an executive playpen for all members of the lucky sperm club. And families must recognize this.

4) **There must be a genuine desire on the part of the owners (a) to create a working board and (b) to take the steps necessary to make sure such a board can carry out its functions.**

Clearly, if The Boss or The Family won't take the board's suggestions seriously, the whole idea of creating an outside board is an exercise in futility (and a costly one, at that). In fact, it will probably only make matters worse by giving each "side" additional gladiators.

This is the most important condition to be met. Realize that outside directors have no real power over an owner-manager. *True legal power in a corporation always rests with its ownership, and in direct proportion to the relative size of that ownership.* Directors can only be effective with an authority that is drawn from the owners' respect for the board, and their *expressed desire to accept and act* on the board's suggestions and advice.

Any successful family-owned business can have a working board of outside directors once it's ready. The only things generally standing in the way are the lack of conviction that such a board is needed, and the lack of determination to go out and create it.

Section II

Creating A Working Board

Chapter 4

What Is an Outside Director

A "working" board isn't just a board that works hard.

When an owner-manager puts together a board consisting of some key employees and maybe a couple of important advisors, he looks at his creation and feels pretty good about it. They meet once in a while, and when they do, they work real hard. So when we talk about a "working" board, sometimes this is what he thinks we mean.

But the real name for this kind of setup is still an "inside" board. The "directors" are all intimately involved with the business in some way or other and, therefore, dependent on the CEO for their jobs, their incomes, and his continued good will.

An inside board like this—even if it is something more than a family picnic—is really nothing more than a management committee meeting with technicians. It's a group with definite value, but it's not a board of directors.

Look at it coldly. It's ridiculous to expect an "inside" board consisting of employees and advisors to evaluate the management, especially the CEO or the other owners. It's also ridiculous to expect them to pass judgement on management policies or decisions. After all, who made those decisions in the first place?

For The Boss to get the kind of review and advice he needs so desperately, he's going to have to find directors who will be able to balance the internal self-interests of the business, the family, and the employees—not directors who add to them or crusade for them. The best candidates for this are people who are engaged in enterprises different from The Boss's business, who both appreciate and understand the risks he shoulders, whose judgement he respects, and who respect him.

The next question, of course, is who fills this bill?

PEOPLE WHO DON'T BELONG ON BOARDS

One good place to begin defining who would be appropriate as an outside director is to determine who is *inappropriate*. In other words, who is not the kind of person we want as a director?

The following judgements aren't made on the basis of prejudice. They're drawn from experience and common sense, both of which tell us that good directors on the board of a family-owned company are *not*:

Professional Advisors or Experts. Attorneys, accountants, consultants, insurance agents, and the like are usually inappropriate because of actual or potential conflicts of interest. Such professionals certainly can and do provide valuable functional tools for management, but their services are otherwise available.

If we need the specific advice of a professional, we should be prepared to buy it and use it, and most good professionals would prefer it that way. They are very often concerned about being forced to transfer their credibility in technical matters, where they are very competent and comfortable, into areas where the real issues generally *are not* within their expertise. And yet, as directors, there they are, expected to say something profound and look wise on subjects outside of their professional knowledge. It's really not fair to them.

Key managers. Insiders (and this can include young successors), when pressed to the wall on the really important decisions, are usually little more than rubber stampers who know how (and when) to "yes" the boss. Their presence on the board also inhibits criticism by whatever outsiders we may be lucky enough to have. The proper involvement of managers is a tactical one, and shouldn't be confused with the strategic role required of a director.

Need a manager's advice? Convene a management meeting. Want his/her opinion or knowledge made available to the board on specific issues? Have them make their reports *to* the board. They don't have to be members—instead they can be a resource invited for the purpose of sharing their specific information. (It really shapes up inside managers to know they are going to have to make a prepared, formal presentation in their field of expertise to outsiders who are going to be judging their performance!)

Retired Ex-employees/Advisors. If there's one thing any Boss doesn't need in his planning process, it's old timers who reminisce about how they used to do it in the good old days. The board surely is no place to sequester seniors out of "gratitude." If a line to the past has value, have specific alumni gatherings and enjoy the memories without having to expect a lot more.

Relatives. Few relatives can offer enough concrete help to outweigh their almost inevitable contribution to squabbles, intrigue, or misunderstanding within the wider family (the business "Mishpocheh").

If the business owner already has a whole group of relatives on the board, he is best advised to get rid of them. There's no purpose in having a professionally oriented board of directors stymied by Uncle Milton, who's convinced if gold still backed the dollar the company could have made some money, or Aunt Sarah Mae, who never will accept why her son (who studied art history in New York and "loved people,") wasn't made sales manager.

The uninvolved minority shareholder/relatives can have some complaints, legitimate or not (Why can't *we* use the company airplane when we travel?), but to burden a directors meeting—which is always too short as it is—with this sort of harrassment is tantamount to calling the meeting off.

People with non-negotiable personal demands or people who continually remind us how good the Good Old Days were are useless, because board members must be people who are able to understand—and become involved in—the days we're going to have to face.

Getting incumbent non-contributors off the board, voluntarily or otherwise, will usually require considerable "creativity," in addition to athletic timing and feather-touch tact like that required of a successful diplomat in the Middle East— but the reward will invariably repay the effort.

Cousin Stanley expects you to listen to his opinion? Better to invite him to dinner.

Friends. "Good Old Days" discussions with friends, too, are best left to the corner pub or a class reunion. A board's attention should be on *tomorrow* . We should wonder, too, how many of our friends would be able to review our behavior objectively? This isn't what we have friends for.

Need a buddy's advice or sympathy? Split a sixpack with him.

Suppliers, Agents, or Customers. Here we come up against severe conflicts of interest. These people, once on our board, will constantly be torn between doing what is best for themselves and what is best for the company—and the choice is heavily loaded in their favor.

Need a supplier's advice, or an agent's? Ask him—or wait. He'll probably give it to you on his own. Need a customers's advice? You probably won't even have to ask—or wait.

Investors. Minority investors are generally inappropriate as board members, because their main function is usually to "represent their interests." While a case could be made for installing an investor *who had qualifications to bring to the board over and above his ownership* , this has proven to be a generally unwise thing to do. Investors suffer from conflict of interest, too, because their concept or objective for gaining a return on their investment may not coincide with the best interests of the business.

People who are involved with a family-owned business solely because of their investment, or "rights" they acquired by inheritance or marriage, should generally find it in *their* best interest to see that the company has the best possible board, with a majority of capable, objective outside directors, rather than one dependent on their own limited contribution. A working board will take good care of those shareholders and their interests by taking good care of their investment, the business.

Many shareholder advocates will resist this—and so will some shareholders ("X% of ownership is *entitled* to a seat on the board," they say). This book is not the place to discuss such legal rights, but it seems to us that these "rights" were granted on the assumption that "shareholders" would be experienced investors whose qualifications would *enhance* the board. This may be true in those instances of publicly owned companies with directors of proven competence who accept their responsibilities seriously, but it has been our experience that most investor/shareholders, who act as directors in their own behalf, "have a fool for a client" (not unlike lawyers who plead their own cases). Even the finest surgeons don't operate on their own family.

Investors' opinions, in most cases, can be better expressed at shareholder meetings or through direct communication with the directors, than by side-tracking directors meetings.

One further point: Allocating tax free "benefits" to minority shareholders in lieu of dividends, even aside from the question of legality, too often creates more and bigger problems. The resulting conflicts often cost more than the usually minor tax "savings" involved, because they divert attention from the most important issue—business survival. It's an amazing experience to see, over and over again, how much static family businesses create for themselves seeking "tax savings" of relatively little dollar value.

Need an investor's advice? Just show him a financial statement and then hold a shareholder meeting.

Spouses. In most cases, our marriage partners—usually Momma—have no place on the board. There are instances, of course, where a wife can be the moving force behind the business and should probably be chairman. But these cases, though increasing in number, are still rare. Usually she's there either because she's "always been there," or because Dad thinks it's a good way to keep her "up to date."

The main purpose of a board meeting, however, is *not* to inform Mother. It is to set policy and otherwise challenge The Boss to reach heights he might not reach alone and without allies.

Yes, Mom *should* know what's going on in the business. But she doesn't have to be a director to find out. She can learn just as efficiently (and probably more comfortably) through regularly scheduled meetings/dinners with the directors and advisors (so they all can get to know each other), or as a *guest* at board meetings. If these really do have substance, she might like to see for herself how good they are.

Need Mom's advice? Ask her—she probably has a lot to say that's worthwhile. Still, it almost seems to be part of the male ego to refuse to believe women can know anything of consequence about business. Fortunately, the current generation is going to help change that archaic prejudice—for the benefit of all concerned. Most men would be a lot better off in a lot of ways if they once learned to listen to their wives.

While, in most cases, board membership would appear to be a recognition of a wife's contribution, actually it's mostly a way to make up for the fact that Mom never gets the facts (and the doubts) straight from The Boss. When there's a family business involved, the need for husband and wife to communicate on business matters as well as on any other subject is fundamental, but too often a wife's board membership is an unsatisfactory "solution" to poor communication. A wife's needs and contributions go far deeper—and are more important—than cursory, symbolic participation in meetings of dubious value.

Leaders in Your Industry. Sure, some heads of similar businesses are non-competitive (too far away), and meetings with them are helpful, but don't confuse technical trade opinion with value judgements.

If you want a competitor's opinion, go to a trade show or association meeting.

In short, inappropriate board members of *all* kinds almost invariably have a negative effect on the boards they inhabit. Overly aggressive pseudo-directors inhibit others who have something to say. Underqualified or incompetent inappropriate directors often end up either being pointedly ignored or else talked down to by the board members who *are* knowledgeable. Even worse, competent directors faced with underqualified fellow board members tend to spend too much time on lengthy explanations, allowing the meeting to degenerate into a class in elementary business.

If this type of activity continues for a long period of time, even the most conscientous director ends up feeling that he's involved in a "One Man's Family" episode of corporate "show 'n"tell." He loses interest, his contribution diminishes, disappears altogether, and eventually he quits.

In all cases, the only criterion for board membership must be *contribution* , not relationship or entitlement.

Given all this, then, who should the business owner consider as prospective board members?

THE BEST DIRECTORS ARE RISK-TAKING PEERS

To have his decisions examined competently in the harsh light of business needs, a business owner must seek the help of a *risk-taking peer*, someone who is *not beholden* to him in any way other than through a moral sense of commitment to what the owners are trying to do with the business.

This is the sort of person who understands the concerns of the business owner, because he also faces the same kinds of challenges, frustrations, problems, trade-offs, joys, and decisions every day.

The outside director is a risk-taking peer who can act as both a devil's advocate and as the business owner's advocate. He is able, through experience and understanding, to analyze and isolate the truth without being polite, and to compliment without being a flatterer.

The risk-taking peer is more than just a burr under the saddle, however. He's a person who genuinely admires the chief executive as a man, who likes him, wants him to succeed, and who is willing to push him to keep trying harder and harder .

He's the kind of person the owner-manager works hard to *deserve* as a director.

THE VIRTUES OF A GOOD DIRECTOR

The business owner should choose outsiders—people *outside* of both his family and his business, *people whose views he can't buy at any price.* Directors should be people who are willing to help the owner manager understand his business better by asking penetrating questions.

A good director must point to the problems as he sees them—and to the tools for their solution. He must inspire management commitment, and guide the CEO's actions, by his own example. The outside director's job is to stimulate the efforts of all involved by demonstrating that the problems are not only soluble, but *worth* solving. More than this he can't do—but if he does less, he fails to fulfil his obligation.

Directors must get top management to ask the right questions, because accepted answers from the past aren't enough. Even if someone were to come to us with the answers to all our unsolved problems, we probably wouldn't understand or listen to him. Answers are only meaningful after our own needs have driven us to raise the questions they solve.

Directors should possess the qualities of unquestioned integrity, proven good judgement, successful problem-solving ability, a personal feeling for the value of action and the requirements of risk management, and a sense of compassion for those involved.

Because business problems of the modern corporation increasingly take on political, social, and economic overtones, directors must have an awareness, a varied perspective, and an adaptability to enable them to understand the changing circumstances of our contempory world. The sort of management decisions which a board must assist the CEO in making require more than expertise in a specific field, industry, or profession.

Board members should be active in business. A person who sits on a board and tolerates the CEO in order to feel needed or useful and active is not a fully helpful board member.

There usually comes a point after a man retires that he needs to prove he's busy. No business owner needs to be a social worker and put people on his board so they have something more

TEN QUESTIONS
TO CONSIDER IN
THE SELECTION OF
OUTSIDE DIRECTORS
...AND ANY OTHERS WHOSE COUNSEL WE SEEK

1. WILL THEY SHARE
   OUR COMMITMENT TO OUR GOALS?

2. CAN THEY COMMUNICATE
   THEIR CONCERNS WITH COMPASSION?

3. IS OUR CONFIDENCE
   IN THEIR COUNSEL JUSTIFIED?

4. CAN THEY COLLABORATE
   EFFECTIVELY WITH OTHERS?

5. IS THEIR COURAGE EVIDENT
   IN TIMES OF DIFFICULTY?

6. DO THEY TRY TO LIVE BY
   THEIR OWN CONVICTIONS?

7. DO THEY HAVE AN INNER
   DRIVE TO CONTRIBUTE?

8. DO THEY RECOGNIZE THE CONTINGENT
   COST TO US OF TAKING THEIR ADVICE?

9. IS THEIR COMPETENCE
   ACCEPTED BY THEIR COLLEAGUES?

10. ARE WE COMFORTABLE
    IN THEIR COMPANY?

...AND SOME
"CONTRIBUTIONS"
WE DON'T NEED
FROM DIRECTORS
...OR ANYONE ELSE,
FOR THAT MATTER

CONFLICT

COLLUSION

CONSPIRACY

CONFRONTATION

...WHICH CAN ONLY LEAD
TO OUR EVENTUAL

COLLAPSE!

stimulating to do with their time than cutting the grass on the bias or bashing golf balls into the rough.

Many retired businessmen aren't effective as board members for very long, because retirement can have an unfortunate tendency to put many men out of touch with the contemporary world. It can deny them an opportunity for continued stimulation and creative problem solving. Retirement can tend to make men concentrate on reliving/embellishing/inventing past achievements, instead of anticipating challenges.

Let us state clearly here, however, that "active" versus "inactive" should *not* be construed as just "young versus old." There are many "oldtimers" who are more active and more contributory in their renaissance careers than they ever were in their original jobs. And there are many young men and women, presumably in the prime of life, who *never* had a responsible thought in their lives (and probably never will). These people retired from the real world years ago, but just haven't been found out.

"Active" should mean that participation on *your* board generates ideas and thoughts that the directors, too, are going to act upon—that the stimulation from your meetings is an invaluable concommitant to their other activities. Your directors are "active" if they *too* are learning all the time. Your meetings must be meaningful to them—both in substance and in the chance they have to associate with the other directors.

To be more specific, an ideal outside director of a family-owned company will be:

1) Someone of proven ability, with outstanding performance in business management or other areas useful to the company.

Proven ability generally means "success," however that's defined in the field the person inhabits. Time has a way of shaking out the blowhards and back-slappers, leaving only those people who have the courage, the staying power, and the talent to survive. A good director, in other words, should be someone who is considered successful by his peers and by most objective standards.

2) Someone whose present position is one of significant responsibility in which risk is an accepted part of the decision-making process.

Responsibility and risk are the daily companions of every successful owner-manager, and they require a very unique set of abilities and understandings. This isn't to imply that someone without a great deal of responsibility, or someone who is exposed to relatively little risk, isn't able. But such people will not usually be able to *appreciate* the business owner's concerns, much less be able to help him solve them.

3) Someone who is absolutely independent of the company he is to direct. There should be no conflict of interest. A director should not be a customer, a supplier, an agent, a relative, or a competitor. Nor should he have potential to be any one of these. For similar reasons, professional advisors (attorneys, bankers, consultants, insurance agents, accountants, etc.) who would normally work for a fee, are also inappropriate for the board. They can be of the greatest help, however, in getting a board started. The best advisors will welcome outside review. They may not get it as often as they'd like, but, generally, they thrive under it.

4) Someone who adds a needed dimension to the board and, therefore, broadens the range of experience and expertise available to the company.

The business owner doesn't need a director who's just like himself. That only multiplies the problem. What he needs is someone who complements his abilities, who adds to his strengths and minimizes his weaknesses. The Boss needs the addition and diversity that directors can bring by virtue of their background (not only business, but also ethnic, religious, or socio-economic), their age (older *and* younger), and their lifestyle. He *doesn't* need the multiplication that would come from a group of people just like him.

5) Someone who is articulate, self-confident, mature, cooperative, and enthusiastic.

Without these qualities, an outside director would never be able to withstand the force of the business owner's personality. Besides, these virtues are almost universal signs of ability. They tend to go along with success. They also make the potential director a joy to have around, because he enjoys being participative and seeks to make a contribution.

6) Someone who is respected by his contemporaries and peers.

When we are looking for successful, talented, able people, we can find few better judges to help us than those who understand and respect ability.

Good advisors can be especially helpful in identifying these kinds of people, because they generally have a wide range of acquaintance with the leaders in many fields of interest and areas of responsibility. It's in the nature of their job to know the winners.

7) Someone who has demonstrated respect for the independent owner-manager as a contributor to our nation's well-being, and has the capability of understanding such an owner's dreams and goals.

We are going to be asking our outside directors to help us achieve a dream. We are going to ask them to help us in ways for which we could never fully compensate them. We are going to ask them to *care* about us, about our business, and about our family. This isn't something we ask of passing acquaintances or people on the street.

There's a lot to be said for the importance of good personal "chemistry," not only with the CEO, but also with the other directors. Harmony among peers rather than competitive one-upsmanship should be the goal.

8) **Someone whose continued respect the owner-manager will want to earn.**

Commitment works two ways, and if The Boss isn't willing to open himself up and to put in the effort his directors are going to require, his board will degenerate into something worse than useless.

None of this is intended to imply that the only person who can be an outside director is another owner-manager. That would be foolishly restrictive because there are so many other people who can contribute what has been described. Another successful business owner, whose talents are respected, can be indispensible on the board of a family company, but many others can also fill the requirements as well.

Professional managers from public companies make excellent outside directors, particularly if they have expertise and experience in areas the company lacks. Such men are also risk-taking peers in the sense that they have built their careers on the discipline of the tough decisions they have made, decisions that required skill, heart, and guts to make—and which, in turn, were judged by the objective standards of others. By the same guidelines, leaders with credentials from the academic community, from trade associations (if different from your own), or government—to name just a few places to look—can work out well.

Good people exist in *many* fields. They stand out, once you accept the need to find them.

A key point to keep in mind is that a qualified, committed outside director, whatever his experience and background, is the kind of person who can sit across the table from the owner-manager, look him square in the eye, and feel comfortable telling him the truth as he sees it.

People such as this can provide a business owner with the required commitment because they understand and love the business life, because they have dedicated their lives to building their dreams, and because they can understand the dreams of others.

People such as this can provide both the compassion and the discipline that are absolutely necessary if the business owner's plans for the future are to be carried out.

Acting in concert as outside directors to the family-owned business, people such as these can provide a solid bridge between generations, between ideas, and between the seemingly insoluble dilemmas that increasingly confront the successful family business.

THE KINDS OF PEOPLE NEEDED

Outside directors are put on boards for very definite reasons. If we look at these reasons for a moment, the sort of person we want on the board will begin to emerge on his own.

A good board of directors will usually help the business owner fill the following needs:

1) **Expanding Financial Knowledge.** Few entrepreneurs are financial wizards. Many aren't even comfortable with financial statements. Yet finance is fundamental to running a growing business. A director (or directors) with a good financial background can increase the CEO's confidence in making the financial decisions that generally accompany all other decisions.

2) **Filling in Weak Spots.** A common disease among successful entrepreneurs is trying to live by the belief that they

can do everything. Common symptoms of the disease are loneliness, harassment, exhaustion, shortage of time, and being increasingly worried about the future. The best cure is a stiff shot of outside help in the form of directors who are good where we are weak.

3) **Handling Growth.** A successful business must grow. It's the only way to make sure change is positive. Yet, left to ourselves, we value "growth" less and less as we age. After all, growth almost always means more work, more energy, more risk. Why play around with what we've got, we ask, for what we don't need? No, *we* don't need growth. We did once, and we did grow. What *we* want now, we tell people, is "controlled growth," to keep up with inflation and the GNP. It's all *we* need.

But growth is always going to be the challenge for those who face the future. Sure, it requires hard work, but that's why we install successor management. That's also why we need a good board to help them and watch them grow. It's just a matter of definition.

There are two kinds of growth, both of which can be helped by good outside directors:

To manage *quantitative growth* —the sheer increase in size and complexity that comes from increased opportunity— many changes in financing, marketing, production, personnel, and operating policies are required. On the other hand, *qualitative growth* —the increase in reputation, recognition, quality, internal skill, and management technique—is much more subtle in its demands than mere increase in physical size. But in many companies it's more important.

The company's experience in either of these kinds of growth might be limited, but others have gone through it before us. Why reinvent the lightbulb? *Experienced* direction can be invaluable.

4) **Amplifying Individual Abilities.** Each successful business owner is truly a genius in his own right. But all genius is limited. If we accept that the whole is greater than the sum of its

parts, we can also accept that an increase in the parts leads to an even greater increase in the whole. Dedicated outside directors, *working together with a motivated owner-manager*, can generate a power far beyond their significant, but individual, contributions as directors.

These are the directors we will need. The existence of such people doesn't guarantee the ultimate success of an outside board, however, because directors don't direct. At best, they stir the CEO and his managers to truly manage.

Directors serve their company best less by the answers they give than by the questions they raise, less by their explicit instructions or impressive credentials than by their example and their commitment, less by their glossing over of difficulties than by their respect for the management's capacity to meet and eliminate these difficulties.

Implementing these board contributions is The Boss's responsibility.

THE "IDEAL" BOARD

Given all of this, how can we create an "ideal" board of outside directors? Below is a useful description, but keep in mind that few successful outside boards will fit this model exactly. This is because competent people tend to be competent in many areas. Their abilities to fill needs overlap.

But, in general, a board of outside directors should consist of:

a) *A person who knows financial management and control better than anyone in the company .*

b) *A person who is strong in The Boss's primary area of weakness, and who is preferably in a comparable rather than identical industry .*

c) *A person who runs a business that has successfully grown the way The Boss wants his to grow .*

d) *A person who is successful in an area into which the business plans to expand .*

e) *A generalist with the energy and personality to spark everybody's best efforts, someone to bring in the offbeat and unexpected .*

It may be that any one person can fill two or more of these "slots," or it may be that several directors have similar characteristics. If so, all the better, as long as they are covered.

A well-structured board will also contain as wide a balance as possible of varying ages, backgrounds, and disciplines (e.g. finance, marketing, production, organization, etc.). A well-designed board will amplify the powers of each individual because it encourages its members to enjoy and to challenge each other.

Add to this group of outsiders a motivated chairman/CEO (or, in the case of two or three mature equal owners, motivated "partners"), and you have an instrument of awesome contribution.

A well-balanced board is a vibrant, living entity, uniquely positioned in the business owner's world.

All it awaits is his desire that it be created.

Chapter 5

How To Put Them Together

A working board isn't put together overnight. It can't even be done over a long weekend. "Directors" can't be looked up in the Yellow Pages. A board has to *evolve* through many important stages.

The first and maybe toughest requirement is The Boss's desire to have a real board—a desire that, too often, just isn't there. Unfortunately, this "lackawanna" doesn't exist as *his* problem (he doesn't see it as a problem because he doesn't feel the need). Instead, it's a problem for the frustrated people around him (usually his successors) who see the need for a board, but don't have the power to create one.

It doesn't matter how many people around the owner-manager see the potential value of an outside board. The desire to have outside directors has just gotta be there in the Boss's mind if a real board is ever going to happen.

But this isn't all. Even after a genuine desire to create a real board exists in The Boss's head, incumbent directors often represent the next major obstacle. Every corporation has them, many of them are inappropriate, and few are in a rush to submit their resignations. Somehow, they must be persuaded to accept their departure with grace—a job that will require consummate *diplomacy*.

There are also a few more requirements: *commitment*, *patience*, *openness*, and a lot of *hard work*.

Commitment, of course, means The Boss "gotta wanna," as a stand-up comic used to say. Others have to "gotta wanna," too, and The Boss must "sell" this idea to his spouse, his successors, his partners, and his key men if he wants their commitment—not just their begrudging, tacit acquiesience.

Patience means The Boss has to be ready for setbacks and frustrations. Good people aren't found everywhere, and even if they're found, they might not be able or ready to serve. He has to learn to express his needs in such a way that prospective directors know what it is he's asking of them.

Openness is probably the toughest part for most business owners. It requires a readiness to open up a part of their lives they've kept closed to others for many, many years.

Hard Work needs no explanation, but if a business owner wants the eventual benefits of a real board for his company, he's going to have to accept the up-front energy costs. That's another reason why there aren't as many working boards around as there ought to be. The Boss knows how to work hard, he just finds it difficult to work hard at something so new and unfamiliar. The spirit *is* willing (sometimes), but the flesh is weak (and getting weaker).

It doesn't take many glances at this list of "requirements" to explain why "outside director" hasn't become a household phrase among family businesses.

GETTING THE BOSS TO "WANNA"

A fact of life, like failing eyesight and postal rate increases, is the almost absolute power of the business owner to do as he damn well pleases. If The Boss doesn't want a board, there isn't going to be a board, thank you.

If you are an *owner-manager* , you don't have this problem. If you did, you wouldn't have read this far.

But if you are a *successor*, a *spouse*, or a *successor's spouse*, or an *advisor* , *supplier* , or anyone else concerned with the continued viability of an owner-manager's business in today's world, there's a good chance that great American hero you know needs a working outside board, but has no time for the idea. That's probably why *you've* read this far.

We get asked over and over again how to go about persuading Ol' Dad (or The Boss, Hizzoner, or The Godfather... you name him) that a board is a good idea for *him* , and our answer is always the same: find out why he objects to the idea, and then answer those objections with understanding, intelligence and compassion. *The Boss isn't going to create an outside board simply because somebody wants him to. He's only going to do it because he realizes it will solve his problems* .

Find out what his problems are. What are his concerns— both in general, and about outside directors? Does he feel his business is different, that nobody could understand? Is he fearful of the reaction of others? Family? Incumbent directors? Key managers? Who? Is he afraid to let peers into his financial and business affairs? Does he think he'll never get back a value equal to the directors fees he invests? Does he feel that nobody would be interested enough in his business to want to serve as a director? Is he worried tht he wouldn't know enough about what to do with directors once he's got them?

These are mentioned just for openers. Whatever his fears really are, *they* are what have to be addressed.

The concerns can be as varied as the business owners having them. In this way, Dad is really not much different from any other tough customer. The salesman has to know what problems the customer has and what he would see as a benefit. The salesman has to do his homework and then *sell solutions, sell benefits, sell answers* .

WHEN EXISTING BOARDS CAN'T BE DISMANTLED

Assuming a business owner wants an outside board, the first issue he typically has to face is the question of what to do with existing inappropriate directors who, for one reason or another, just aren't removable.

This problem is most commonly faced by successors who inherited an inappropriate board along with the business. These directors can often be the result of an earlier generation's desire to broaden the "loyalty" base of the company, an objective too often sought through the profligate distribution of unrestricted stock. Founders aren't immune, but these "thorns" don't usually develop their really sharp edges until after The Boss has gone on to the Great Reward.

Who are these people? First and foremost among the more typical bad appointments is Mom. It's too easy to ask a good wife to be a legal nonentity, and few business founders resist the temptation. When the successor inherits "Her Directorness," however, she's got tenure—plenty of it. She's been on the board since the beginning, and her position has become her main symbol of control over her destiny—especially if she doesn't work in the business. She's likely to feel that her directorship keeps her current on events within the company, and sometimes she also thinks it's her ticket to deductible travel.

Even if she does "work" in the business, typically her current scope of responsibility is so narrow as to be insignificant, or just narrow enough to cause the successor a real headache.

Often, the early essential contributions of spouses deteriorate over time as the needs of the company—and their own needs/energy—change.

Trouble is, telling her this and attempting to remove her from the board would hurt her deeply, and she is, after all, our wife/mother. If she also happens to also own some or all of the marbles, removal will also be impossible without her consent.

Mom's not the only one, though, whose "removal" (even if possible) would have serious implications. There are many other kinds of entrenched directors—former retired employees and/or their spouses, minority shareholders (or their representatives), children not involved in the company, self-seeking vendors of goods and services, and even Grandmother.

All of these are people who have roots deeply set in the company and on the board, and to attempt to blast some of them out of their seats would often produce more rubble than clearing.

A paraphrase of an old saying seems appropriate: "Let us have the courage to change what can be changed, the grace to accept what cannot be changed, and the wisdom to know the difference."

Does this mean owner-managers with firmly entrenched inappropriate boards have to give up on the idea of a real board?

Well, yes and no.

A TEMPORARY "PRO TEM" BOARD

Every new president, whether in the White House or in a family business, quickly recognizes the effective limits on his power. If certain people just can't be moved or removed, that's generally a fact to be accepted and dealt with. But it doesn't leave the president helpless.

Sometimes it's possible to "pack" the court—i.e. just plain add three or four new directors to the existing body (better first check your by-laws with your legal counsel, however). Once this is done, "full" board meetings are just held once a year to satisfy the legal requirements, while the quarterly meetings are held only with the "executive committee" of the board—which (coincidentally) just happens to consist of the outside directors and the boss. For all intents and pruposes, this can sometimes be the best of all temporary worlds for the beleaguered—but in control—Boss who doesn't have the heart, guts, or power to clean house, but wants to let time take its course without losing the help he needs.

It's a little cumbersome, and could be misconstrued by those opposed to being eased out, but it has proven to be a viable option.

Another option is the creation of an informal, quasi, "pro tem" board of outsiders functioning as a body with all the qualities of a working outside board except the legal sanctions. This is a body of outsiders who understand the situation and are willing to function as an "ad hoc" committee of advisors pending the removal of an entrenched board that can't be "packed."

There are weaknesses with this second approach, of course, but they aren't so great as to outweigh the benefits. Remember that such outsiders fill two very important functions. First, they can act as a body that can advise and assist in the continuity of management direction in the event of tragedy. Second, they can provide a forum of competent, understanding peers against whom the owner-manager can check his judgments and decisions on a wide range of topics, including the review of his successor management planning and development.

It's true that management continuity can be provided best by a formally constituted legal entity called a board of directors. They have the power to *direct*. Others can only advise. But a "pro tem" board of advisors can still help with continuity in the face of tragedy, even though not as effectively as a full outside board, because it makes available the expertise and commitment of the informed outsider.

A pro tem board of advisors can also provide the forum of risk-taking peers that's so important to taking some of the loneliness out of the CEO's job. For this function alone, such a board can be immensely useful.

While the facts of company organization, particularly in the matter of the existing directors, how they meet, and how they act, may have to be accepted if they cannot be reasonably changed, there are often some creative ways to get around them when it becomes necessary.

It's up to the incumbent Boss to decide whether the reward is going to be worth the effort.

DEFINING THE AREAS OF NEED

Let's make the major assumption, however, 1) that the business owner really *wants* a board and 2) that whatever legal or personal problems he might have with the incumbents *can* be solved. He still faces a number of preliminary questions which he must answer before he can start putting together his actual board of directors.

The first step taken, long before a CEO goes out to recruit directors, is to define just what it is he wants to accomplish with the board. What is it supposed to do? These objectives, once they're defined, will be the foundation on which he will build the form and structure of his board.

There are *many* roles a board can fill, but no single board can do everything. It's not enough just to state some general objective such as "the board should protect the company's financial integrity," or "it should assure smooth succession," Vague phrases like these might sound impressive, but they really don't say anything useful. The owner-manager, based on his perceived needs and the experience gaps within the company, must himself define the *specific* areas where he needs help in sharing his load as a risk-taker.

And his load changes with time. For companies in early stages of development, it is more important to seek a director who has the experience, maturity, and self-confidence to *assist in*, as well as *review*, the owner-manager's decisions and actions. He should be able to be both a friendly advisor *and* a challenge to the business owner. In a sense, the early board functions much like an outside management committee.

But as the company grows, the director's role becomes increasingly more demanding. As companies grow, conflict tends increasingly to add to the constant need for attention to business requirements.

And board structure should reflect these changing requirements.

Once the specific areas of risk management are defined, the next step is to decide on the specific kinds of expertise and experience which would be useful in a director.

If, for example, financial actions, such as managing increasing debt, anticipating changes in capital structure, or establishing new means of fiscal control are to be a major duty of the board, someone with a strong financial background might be needed.

Or, if the company is also facing some long-range marketing decisions or diversification plans, one or more directors well experienced in such decisions and risks could be very useful.

The directors selected should be people well equipped to handle the responsibilities the owner-manager feels the company will face, but, since directors are asked to supply broad direction, covering many different areas of management, it could be argued that any given director's specific area of expertise is irrelevant to his job. The trouble with this argument is that it's wrong. Nobody is able to work solely as an objective filter of information. Every director will have a specific bias through which he interprets what he's told. Wouldn't it be best to *choose* that bias as something needed by the company?

WHERE ARE GOOD DIRECTORS FOUND?

Potential directors are all around. They belong to trade and professional organizations, they work with us on community projects or in church groups, they are found in meetings and projects, and seminar groups of all description. *What we have to do is learn to talk with them, to get to know them, and to let them get to know us* .

Once a potential director is found, the process is a lot like courtship. But finding candidates seems to cause the greatest difficulty for most owner-managers.

Men with the required qualifications aren't discovered overnight. Good directors are like good spouses—they must be found where we live. We must become sensitive to the fact that people we need do exist. We must meet them to know—and, eventually, ask—them.

Many people feel reluctant to get close, on a business basis, to people they've met on some other basis. Mostly the only people they know are already involved in their business in some way. They're either customers, suppliers, advisors, friends, investors, or old buddies in the clubs and trade association. But we would all probably agree that people like this are rarely objective about either the company or its management.

But people do exist, everywhere, who are sympathetic and willing to share a commitment to the goals of others. We have only to ask them, and be willing to share our hopes and concerns with them, to allow them to see where the problems are, where we want to go, what our strengths are, and what our weaknesses are.

This is the problem, though. Most people won't be that open with anyone. Too many are economic atheists. They believe only in themselves. They feel no one can help them. By their choice, they suffer alone.

The typical family corporation CEO would have a difficult time trying to name three outsiders with whom he would be willing to be completely frank. But, then, if he is not going to be honest, why should he bother with the fiction of a board?

The usual escape phrase is something like: "My business is different. Outsiders don't understand my problems." This is because the owner manager considers their facts "opinions," while his opinions are "facts." That's the *real* problem.

An owner-president can become his own worst enemy. He permits the income that has been generated by his company over his lifetime to fool him into thinking that he always knows what he is doing, and that no one else does or ever did or ever can. Or so he thinks. How can he really know, since he never competed for the job? It's not hard to anoint ourselves under conditions of personal success.

Potential board members are everywhere. They can be found among the people with whom we associate. It's necessary, however, for the president of the closely held company continually to enlarge his circle of acquaintances, rather than to depend upon the same group of people who have influenced him in the past.

By participating in seminars and by serving on boards of local business, civic, and charitable organizations, company presidents can become acquainted with their peers in problem-solving situations, and thus reduce their essentially parochial view of outsiders, their contributions, and their very existence.

What the business owner needs to develop is an economic parallel for the biological/spiritual drive that keeps us looking for the right girl to marry.

The president must look for people who are worthy of trust, people esteemed professionally and ethically, people who are interested in contributing. He must look for people who are able to enlarge his present concepts of management, successful people with good reputations. He needs people with courage, confidence, and curiosity—questioners and participants, not just passive listeners.

HOW TO JUDGE A POTENTIAL DIRECTOR

There are a number of important considerations when evaluating the quality and usefulness of a potential director. Impressions are important, of course. There is something called "personal chemistry" that becomes obvious, sometimes even on the first meeting, and if that good rapport doesn't exist, there's little chance this person will work out well as a director for our company.

But there are more things we should look at than just how well we seem to get along.

1) **Background.** It's important to learn as much as possible about the history and experience of a potential director. This isn't something that can be done through resumes or interviews, however. The relationship we're looking for with this person is too broad and deeply based for that.

The important issues in a potential director's background include much more than what he's done—although that's important, of course. What we want to know is what kind of person he is, based on the sorts of experiences he's had.

For example, has this man has ever *failed* at anything? There's nothing like some past failure for building character and teaching the important lessons. (As someone once said, "good judgement comes from experience, and experience comes from bad judgement.") While failure, per se, shouldn't, by any means, be a requirement for a directorship, when it has happened to someone, it can tell us a lot about that person. What did he learn? How did/does it affect him now?

We should ask whether our potential director understands *real risk* . What kinds of risks has he taken and how well has he done? A lot can be learned about a man by looking at the ventures he's involved in. They tend to define the extent of his talent, the depth of his courage, and even the breadth of his optimism.

We should discover the *source of this person's success* . Upon what has he built his influence and his reputation? Is it real? This latter question can be very important, because often what looks like success is merely cosmetic.

A man's *relationship to his family* is usually a good indication of his value system. There is little question that a stable home contributes to a stable and positive outlook.

Finally, we should decide whether or not we *respect* what this person has done. It's one thing to be impressed by a person's accomplishments, and an entirely different thing to feel those accomplishments are important and worthwhile.

2) **Present Occupation.** We should determine the real nature of what this potential director does in his everyday activity. It's important to be as exact about this as possible, because this will define the sort of help and advice we will be able to draw upon once—and if—this person is on our board.

If the potential director is a business owner, we should find out everything we can about his business. What is it? How does he perceive it? How does he see its relationship to our business? If he is a professional manager or an authority in other fields, what are his special responsibilities and skills? Where, in short, can his experience be *specifically* helpful to us in our business?

3) **Opinions of Others.** We should determine what other people think about this potential director. Obviously, this is something to be done informally—a potential director is not a job-seeker.

We should ask who knows this man? Whom does he know? What is his wider reputation in the community? In the business world? Who are his friends? Who—if we can find this out—are his enemies? (All successful people will have a few, and they can help greatly in defining a person) How much will the opinion others have for this person affect our company if he joins our board.

4) **Opinions of Present Directors.** Present board members, good or bad, can offer additional insight into potential directors. After all, these newcomers are their replacement, and we all like to feel it takes somebody special to replace us.

All candidates should meet each of the present directors so that each can come to his own conclusion about the potential director. This is especially important when we attempt to restructure an existing "family" board composed of father, mother, brother, sister, and the like. For the most part, existing directors will each think they "add" or "watch" something, and do so with an unique personal insight. Meeting potential directors can have a beneficial effect in that reasonable people will usually realize that their contribution can be made better through the presence of an objective surrogate, with no ax to grind, than by personal involvement. Only excessively egocentric inappropriate directors will insist on personal representation once they have met real flesh and blood examples of committed, competent and contributory directors.

If we should be so fortunate as to already have one or two "real" directors, nobody will have a better understanding of us and our needs than they would. Few people could serve as better judges of the potential usefulness of future outside directors.

ASKING THE CANDIDATE TO SERVE

Once the right people have been found, the most effective way to get them on our board is to come right out and ask them. The request itself is a vote of confidence, as well as an expression of respect. (Contrary to uninformed opinion, most people with the qualifications needed in a good outside director would be challenged and flattered by a request to serve on the board of a successful family company.)

For example, one good way both to use the knowledge of our professional advisors and to find good directors, is to ask each of our advisors to give us their recommendations, to help us select people with experience in the areas we need to have covered.

Realize that these are very flattering recommendations, and will be quickly seen as such by the selected people. Say our attorney, account, or banker recommends someone. A good approach is to contact this person and tell him our advisor thinks he's one of the most competent business people in town. What better reason to want to meet him?

If we do this with each of the candidates we've found, at worst, we'll have a chance to meet a group of stimulating people. At best we're almost certain to find among them three or four or five who seem to have that important light behind the eyes that indicates they might be great potential outside directors for us.

It's to this latter group of outsiders that we will want to express our needs. It's not a particularly good idea to tell everyone we're looking at that we want to put together a board and they're a candidate. This could prove embarrassing should the person not work out. But once we've played the field and narrowed the list down to the few people we know we want, we're ready to begin the courtship.

Getting a potential director excited about the idea of serving on a family business board is not as difficult as it may seem at first glance. Most business people have an inbred curiosity about other businesses. They also have an inbred love of business. All we have to do is use these attitudes to generate excitement about *our* businesses. This shouldn't be hard—after all, we are excited about what we do, or we wouldn't be doing it. All that's needed is to explain our business to this potential director in such a way that they can learn to love it in much the same way we do.

When the time seems appropriate to discuss fees, remember that we're trying to acquire commitment, not "services." These people are not selling their services. They have good jobs. They're not being offered an opportunity for moonlighting to increase their standard of living or to pay off old debts. The directors fee should be considered as a symbol that we are taking this relationship as seriously as we are asking them to. It's an integral part of defining the relationship we're looking for, and should be made clear as early as comfortable in the discussion to avoid misunderstanding.

Finally, some thought has to be given to the possibility of rejection. For many reasons, not everyone will be able to serve as an outside director. Often, there's not enough time available to do the job justice. Sometimes there are legal or contractual restrictions on a person's outside activities, or unrealized conflicts of interest.

Whatever the reason, refusals are to be expected. The important point to remember is that, even if our request is turned down, the honor the proposal bestows, as well as the acquaintanceship, remain. It might be that a directorship can become acceptable in the future. It might be that this person would be willing to serve as an informal advisor to the board that is finally formed. It might also be that this person will have some ideas about others who could serve.

The prospect of a directorship in a family-owned company is more attractive than most business owners think. Acceptance rates are generally high. Even if the person who's being asked cannot serve, the business owner, by asking, has widened his circle of acquaintences and made a potentially valuable friend. Once the initial shyness and feeling of "talking out of school" is overcome, a search for directors becomes a new and continuing facet of an owner's perspective. It never goes away. We learn that all we must do is to ask—and be honest and open—and people will be honored by our faith in them. Often they are the ones who are "embarrassed" at our openness and admire us for it.

HOW MANY DIRECTORS?

Too many members on the board restrict its effectiveness. Too few limit its diversity. The actual number of directors is an individual requirement which must be worked out by The Boss as chairman. In general, though, the more people on the board, the better—up to the point at which participation becomes difficult.

The board of a family company should contain enough members to provide diversity. Five is much better than three, but more than six or seven is usually too cumbersome to be effective. The size, complexity, and needs of the company are the determining factors.

Five is a good number—not because it's an odd number, but because it's a good, *manageable* number. Having a greater number increases the the chances that board meetings will deteriorate into mass harangues. With less than five, a single absence would make a bridge game impossible, much less a directors meeting.

Whatever the total number of members, the most important factor is that there should be as much mixture as possible in areas of expertise, background, business affiliation, age, and special talent. While any given closely held company might differ from others in the nature of its specific products, markets, and management styles, most of its problems are faced every day by other businesses, and the people who will best understand the owner/CEO and his goals are other such businessmen.

Remember, to be effective, an outside director needs the confidence of numbers. Token outsiders are easily overwhelmed. Outsiders should be the majority on the board, not outnumbered by the owner-manager and his cronies.

Limiting board participation to the CEO and his Number One Lieutenant would probably be best. If there are two partners involved, then the two of them would be the best insiders. Probably up to three "partners" would be okay, too (we're not trying to force anybody out), but with the addition of more than three or four outsiders, we're beginning to oversize the board.

Companies with multiple owners/investors have to come to grips with the fact that all of them can't be on the board. Five 20% owners, for example, need to accept the fact that their ownership may be equal, but their management contribution is not. Rotate numbers two, three, four, and five on the board, if you must, but outsiders have to deal with *management leaders*, not a shareholders meeting. This is something minority shareholders' (and their spouses) sometimes find hard to accept.

HOW LONG SHOULD A DIRECTOR SERVE?

Tenure on the board is not for life, and this should be made clear at the time of the offer to join. One of the first duties of the formal board should be to set a policy of membership tenure so that removal does not become a personal matter later. After three or four years on a board, members lose their freshness and flexibility, and their utility diminishes. Also, new members provide new insights and keep the president/owner stimulated to articulate his basic concepts.

The precise length of a director's term depends on a number of factors unique to the individual business. Among these factors are:

1) **The Rate of Change in the Industry.** If the environment we inhabit is very fluid and very changeable, tenure on our board has relatively little value, and might even be dangerous. The faster things are changing, the more valuable will be new blood among our directors.

2) **Complexity of the Business.** The more difficult it is to understand our company, the longer should be the director's term. The reason for this should be clear. If it takes a relatively long time for a new director to get to reach the needed understanding, we are only throwing away his true value by rotating him off the board too quickly.

3) **Age of the Board.** As an outside board becomes established, it becomes more stable and able to handle changes in its membership. A new board will have a lot of growing pains and probably will require longer director terms. Established boards can accommodate change their membership more easily.

4) **Need for Continuity.** Clearly, directors terms shouldn't be set in such a way that the directorships all expire at the same time. When a new board is being created, the best approach is to set different tenures for each of the first directors so that rotation comes on a staggered basis. Once the original board has been replaced, set term lengths would become appropriate.

5) **Length of Director Usefulness.** The value of an outside director does not increase forever with time. In fact, a director's useful lifespan is more of a curve—he takes a while to get up to speed, spends a certain time at his peak of usefulness, then begins

to decline in effectiveness. Judging the slope and length of this curve is not easy, but it must be done so that a reasonable directorship term can be determined.

6) **The Desires of the Outside Directors Themselves.** Often, the existence of a time limit on directorships can be an inducement to otherwise hesitant prospective directors. It can allow them the satisfaction of contribution without either the ultimate difficulties attendant to unplanned or undiscussed discontinuance, or the feeling of entrapment without release.

It's usually a good idea to make a retiring director responsible for initiating the search for his replacement, but the ultimate decision always rests with the shareholders. They would be well advised, however, to seek the concurrence of their current directors in each replacement.

HOW SHOULD DIRECTORS BE PAID?

Compensation should always be decided upon before the potential directors are approached.

Some company presidents think that paying a few hundred dollars per meeting is good enough. It isn't.

Payment should be significant. Amounts anywhere from $2000 to $10,000 per annum or more per director for participation in four directors meetings a year are not out of line. Even though the people chosen as prospective directors do not need the money as "income," they are people who have learned to respect compensation and will tend to return value for value. Token payments too often encourage token performance.

The yearly retainer should also be paid irrespective of attendance—perhaps the best way to assure attendance.

Compensation adds a formal and professional dimension to the relationship. Obviously, per annum compensation should be influenced by company size. A $2 million retailer's needs and ability to pay for those needs are far different from those of a $100 million manufacturing business.

The key factor in choosing the exact amount is the significance of the amount to both the offerer and to the acceptor.

Somehow, paying this kind of money, which is not all that great an annual sum—about the price of an additional clerk—also makes the boss pay attention. After all, he's paying to hold this meeting.

Although no owner can hope to compensate at true value for the service that real board members will provide, significant compensation is mandatory for a person of this ability, who offers his time and thought as a director.

Obviously, the quality of this person's contribution is not influenced by the amount of money he's paid, especially since his opinions are not normally for sale, and his contributions to the CEO are non-purchasable. But payment impels both the recipient and the donor to make special efforts to justify the explicit assumption of mutual responsibility and trust.

Directors should be paid in money, not some "creative" tax avoiding benefit (cars, travel, or the gift or use of company assets for personal use). Amounts or deals like this don't impress anybody, nor make them feel especially responsible—just conspiratorial. It also should go without saying that any out of pocket costs of travel, lodging, etc. are the additional responsibility of the company.

As a "reminder," the directors' retainers should be mailed to them 30 days or so before the meeting, or sent with the advance materials the directors need to review.

At these fee levels, it's more likely that the president will prepare himself well so that the meetings are not a waste of time (and money). It's more likely, too, that he'll listen to what is said.

For this kind of money ($2000 to $6000 per meeting in total cost), CEO's feel compelled to do *their* homework, preparing adequate and timely information for the directors, making sure that time, place, and agenda items are confirmed well ahead of time.

For this kind of money, directors, on their part, will realize that the president/owner is serious, and they'll not willingly disappoint him by non-attendance, non-preparation, or superficial thinking. They will want to be considered worthy of their responsibility and consideration.

Payment in advance, as a mutually agreed upon symbol of performance, has an unbelieveably positive effect on serious successful people. They don't want to be considered unworthy of the trust being placed in them. (Only the unsuccessful or insecure, it seems, feel that they're entitled to whatever they can get, irrespective of the resulting obligations placed on them.)

WHY WOULD ANYONE ACCEPT?

One question that is inevitably asked in any conversation about the formation of outside boards is: "why should anyone accept a directorship in a family-owned business?" It seems, for example, that the kind of person who would qualify will be so involved and so busy that this extra responsibility would be adding way too much. Or maybe it seems that since the president "owns" the company, whatever he, the director, says isn't going to make any difference anyway. The excuses go on: why should they take on a legal responsibility for someone else's company? or they really have no financial interest in the company, etc., etc., etc...

Well, people do accept directorships, and for a variety of reasons.

If an owner-manager has built a company which enjoys the respect of its suppliers, customers, and competitors, then service on that business owner's board of directors can be a matter of both pride and challenge for someone invited to serve.

In other cases, directors agree to serve because of the stimulation it offers. Many executives find that serving on the boards of other companies enhances their own knowledge and understanding, enabling them to become better managers in their own companies.

Finally, many people have enjoyed a good and noble life from their experience in the world of business. One way of repaying the debt they feel to those who aided them in their quests is to provide their own time, service, energy, and commitment to insure the survival and growth of the dreams of others, and, thus, to make the world of business a continually better world. There are many fine people who sincerely feel that "you got to give as good as you get."

Really good people are not selfish, or greedy, or continually self-serving. People who feel everybody is just looking out for a buck, or who are out only to upgrade the quality of their friends, are to be avoided.

Compensation is rarely a factor in the acceptance of a directorship. The men who accept them rarely need the money and there is no way to compensate these men for what they have to offer. Nevertheless, money has always accompanied a contract, for it represents a measurable symbol of mutual commitment.

Just as it's true that all the women a man may ask to marry him don't accept, all those asked to be directors may not necessarily accept. Some will genuinely feel that they cannot afford the time required for preparation and attendance at meetings. Others might feel that service on some boards would create a conflict of interest, put them in a position of self-gain or create an atmosphere of competitive advantage.

Sometimes good people refuse board directorships for fear of the personal liability involved in suits against the company. Our experience over 20 years holds overwhelmingly that honest men, acting openly and knowledgeably in consort with other honest men need have little fear on this score. Obviously, there always is a chance that one can become innocently involved in such litigation. In today's world, you can't completely escape liability for any conceivable action. Almost every time we move, act, associate, marry, have children, drive a car, own a dog, or even just inhabit the environment, we face a risk—sometime miniscule, sometimes significant—of landing in court.

This fear of involvement is grossly overstated, and can usually be minimized through a "hold harmless" clause in the company by-laws or meeting minutes, as well as by purchasing insurance protection against director's liability.

If a prospective director has any question as to the character, reputation, or stability of the inviting company or its management, he will surely decline the invitation. In these circumstances, his being a director would only be a detriment to the company. His disapproval of its business policies or belief that its management is incompetent or in an unnecessary state of flux, would render him fundamentally uncooperative.

If too many refusals come up, *you* might have serious cause for examining *your own* reputation and *your* actions.

Chapter 6

Working with Outside Directors

Unlike most other divine beings, the business owner needs advice. He may have to stoop down to listen as it's whispered in his ear, but listen he must.

We run into a lot of confusion, however, about the kind of advice this Great American Hero needs, particularly the kind of advice he should be getting from his board of directors. Historically, boards have acted as *trustees* for the shareholders rather than as *advisors* to the CEO. In the family-owned business, however, the active business owner's greatest needs from his directors are candor, advice, review, and support. These two

114

roles are too often confused, the usual mistake being to confuse management advice with advice on managing management.

If this sounds like doubletalk, consider the fact that every CEO faces problems on two separate levels. First, there are his management problems—such questions as marketing, quality control, money management, materials, personnel, and so forth. These generally are specific questions, usually related to a specific industry or to a specific company size. Their answers, while complex, are generally specific and obtainable from specialists.

MANAGING THE PROCESS OF MANAGEMENT

But the owner-manager, as a CEO, also faces the problem of *managing the process of business ownership itself*. This is a much fuzzier area, dealing as it does with questions of risk, which are specific to each situation. The answers to risk questions may seem uncomplicated, once they're reached, but the process of reaching them is terribly difficult. These are questions whose answers depend mostly on judgement and experience—expert advice can help, but it is seldom the *whole* answer. It's in this latter role that a true working board of outsiders will come into The Boss's life.

Successful business founders generally are not professional managers. Professional managers usually manage other people's businesses—they don't start their own. As an entrepreneurial venture grows, however, the entrepreneur finds that his genius is getting stretched to the limit.

Emerging from the days of the one-man show, the business founder finds that there's a need to start formalizing what was up until this point a really vague—albeit rosy—picture of the future. Often, he doesn't really recognize this, exactly. More likely he finds himself confused, frustrated, limited by facts and events. But the problem, almost universally, is the increasingly obvious lack of management tools—controls, budgets, and the like—as well as a forum in which to discuss them and a management team to put them into place.

All of these tools are likely to be beyond the founder's expertise and experience. His problem isn't that he couldn't create these tools. He is, after all, brighter than most. No, the problem is that nothing in his experience sets him up to be able to *accept* these needs. Here is where his outside directors can prove to be a great advantage.

BOILERPLATE AND THE BOARD'S LEGAL DUTIES

Boards have legal duties and responsibilities, of course, which should be well known to most any competent corporate attorney. Every business owner should at least have a passing familiarity with them, and should make it a policy to clear these areas routinely with corporate counsel *before* the fact. That's why we have corporate counsel.

There are so-called "boilerplate" requirements, for example, that the board approve decisions on compensation, dividends, election of officers, capital formation, and so forth. These requirements are in the bylaws. Read them.

Also, the law in most states will place requirements and responsibilities on the individual director. Generally, state laws will require that a director must:

1) Exercise the same judgment and care in directing the company that any businessman would show in similar circumstances, including the direct questioning of actions of the company which he feels are improper (the so-called "prudent man" consideration), and

2) Refrain from taking specific actions as a member of the board which would by intention result in his own personal gain.

But legal duties and responsibilities, while very important, are not the core areas of the board's importance to the owner-manager. There are many other, non-legal functions which the business owner will find more valuable, if not downright priceless, to him.

THE WAYS A BOARD CAN HELP THE MOST

There are at least five other kinds of support which directors can offer to the president/CEO of a company:

1) **A good director can share his valuable perception of the general business environment with the owner-manager, widening the field of view seen through The Boss's once very necessary blinders.**

One of the most amazing and gratifying phenomena to watch is the process of a capable board discussing the economy, the market, and the future. By themselves, each of the directors is an expert in some sub-area of the economy. Together, these people are able to make ideas grow as they compare, defend, and adjust their individual opinions against the opinions of other respected directors. In this synergistic process, everybody benefits—especially the business owner, to whose business the discussion refers.

If they've been chosen wisely, outside directors will meld into a combination of interests, all dedicated, by choice, to solving the problems and seizing the opportunities, short and long range, inherent in your specific business. Assuming he's installed four outsiders, whose average age might be 45 (some older, some younger, of course), a business owner can be the beneficiary of 100 mature years of experience and exposure, of successes and failures, of traditions and strong feelings—tempered by a sense of commitment unaffected by self-interest. Only a fool would not be impressed by the strength of the instrument he has forged.

2) **A good director can make his specific skills available to the business owner—skills which were acquired over many years of education, experience, and exposure.**

In many ways, a capable director functions as an itinerant professional manager, donating his knowledge and experience as needed, filling requirements as they arise.

We all try hard to find and keep key managers with the skills necessary to operate our businesses. Those skills can run the gamut from sales to statistics, from production to promotion, from accounting to advertising, from R&D to EDP. Our managers (we hope) are the best we can find to run our business, but where can we—or they—go for help in finding objective guidance in our chosen field? Wouldn't it be great to be able to have an objective review on the merits of our, or our team's plans and projections, to make sure that in our optimism (or doubt), our haste (or foot-dragging), our concentration (or dilution) of effort, that we didn't overlook (overemphasize) something that mattered.

Good, working, objective outside directors, each of whom has taken a different road to success than ours, can be invaluable in filling in the gaps of knowledge available within our management team and our advisors.

3) **A good director can encourage (to put it mildly) the business owner to put together the policies and plans needed for the future of his company—and to put those plans into effect.**

We have seen this happen over and over again. Good directors take their responsibility for corporate continuity very seriously, and they know that continuity won't happen by itself. Since they aren't befogged by any sense of the present owner's immortality or omnipotence, they have a very great tendency to push for long-range planning.

It's very easy for all of us, in our passion to solve current crises, to overlook, underemphasise, or just plain disregard the needs of our future. Long range planning, for the typical owner-manager, usually consists of not much more than the attempt to remember to get the brakes checked on his car before the weekend, or to find a substitute for a member of his Saturday foursome in time to qualify for the big match.

After a steady diet of day by day crisis decisions on an ever widening (it seems) range of activities, after the daily discipline over so many years of balancing problems among customers, creditors, and checkbooks, the business owner subconsciously procrastinates on preparing for any problems the future might hold. Here's where a good board will offer him their support and encouragement. His future will soon become his present, and with their help he'll be ready and looking forward to it.

4) **A good director can provide capable, understanding help in times of crisis, helping maintain some objectivity while developing strategies for dealing with the problems.**

This function is important enough during the typical crises business owners face day to day, but it's most important in crises which involve the absence or disability of the owner-manager himself. A board has both the understanding *and the formal authority* to manage the continuity of a business in the absence of the CEO. In many family companies, this power alone has assured continuity of a company that, without an outside board, would have died.

All death is untimely. All disability is tragic. And neither is suceptible to preventive medicine. Tragedy can strike without warning and usually without cause, but too many companies assume that youth and good health and prayer are sufficient shields against it. These strategies may each be helpful, but a sound contingency management would be better—something that's very rare in a privately held company.

The Lord knows it's difficult enough to get one good CEO without having one understudying in the wings, and it's precisely here where a good board can act—decisively, calmly, objectively, and with the right to do so. Many a widow, and many a wife of a disabled owner-manager has had reason to give heartfelt thanks to the existance of a committed and compassionate board of directors in times of tragedy. Many a youthful, instant successor to the job of CEO has had his outside directors to thank for their support in the sudden realization of his responsibilities.

Ultimately, however, the single most important job of the director in the family corporation is what we will list as his fifth task:

5) A good director will help to provide for the profitable continuity of the company.

The most important requirement for continuity is management development—plans must be made to allow for the passing of the torch from the founder's generation to the successor generation. A board is invaluable in helping bridge both the generation gap and its attendant problems in communicating goals to the young. It can also help assure both the competence of the successor and the support of his family.

Whether the predecessor president retires or dies on the job, the new president will need a working board to help him. If the board is familiar with past corporate policies and has been actively engaged in planning and measuring performance against these plans, it can give a lot of assistance to the successor management team. The board is a policy setter, not an after-the-fact operation.

A working board of objective outsiders, from the moment of creation, will be watching for potential successors and leaders—among the heirs, among their spouses, and among the younger key managers (whom good CEO's should recognize as their "business sons," their sons by adoption).

Watching their progress (or lack of it) over the years, the board as a body will get to know well these young managers and their spouses—as well as their hopes and dreams, motivation and ability, commitment and accommodation to each other.

Without an ax to grind—or a potentially biasing relationship—directors can make the necessary objective choices. Everyone in the family—fathers, mothers, siblings, cousins, in-laws, and managers should be relieved and comforted by this impartiality of outside directors in their selection process. All the truly competent successor managers we've known (and their spouses) were always willing (delighted) to be judged *fairly and impartially* —on their merits.

The board must be innovative. It must take the wider view, looking imaginatively at tomorrow. It should challenge the imagination of management and stimulate fresh outlook. Without such a challenge, even the most successful business will come to a point of stagnation. Their managers will have no ideas left. They'll eventually find themselves waiting for the mail to come in to have something to do.

A working board of directors can be a major spur, putting pressure on the CEO to set goals, timetables, and responsibilities. It can offer constructive objectivity in the complex father/son and Boss/employee relationships. It can be a vehicle to pressure a father who won't quit. It can be a vehicle to cajole a founder into training his successor. It can be a stimulus to aspiring successors to "shape up"—to solve the problems they've been given and to upgrade the skills they possess for the needs of the future.

It can be the collective "Solomon" who judges wisely among rival factions. It can be the counsel both to the ambitious and the unmotivated. It can be a lot of things. While it is true that the board's primary responsibility is acted on at board meetings held quarterly or as needed, good directors delight in interim relationships with the various members of the business "mishpocheh"—family, shareholders, successors, and managers. This can be the most challenging, demanding, and satisfying part of the job.

The Boss tends to equate success with survival, but a good board will know he is wrong. It will recognize when he is mostly just treading water. A good board of directors, committed to a man they esteem and respect, can help him see the true danger of this state of affairs before he drowns not only himself, but all of those people who have attached themselves to him.

HOLDING MEETINGS THAT WORK

The chairman of the board of directors should be the incumbent president/CEO. It is his duty to preside at meetings and make them worthwhile. It is up to him to decide on the number of meetings, their length, their location, and their agenda.

A board should meet periodically if it's going to contribute significantly to the operation, normally four times a year. Once the president has decided how often the board will meet and who will be on the board, he should pick fixed meeting dates a year in advance, at regularly scheduled intervals (for example, the first Monday after the quarterly financial statements can be made available). Meetings held much more often than quarterly tend to deteriorate into operational sessions, and meetings held less often than quarterly are almost the same as doing nothing at all. It takes so long to catch up on where we were, on what happened, and why it happened, that it's usually time to go home before the dog and pony show is over. The future never gets discussed.

One of the best reasons for regularly scheduled meeting dates (e.g. March 8, June 7, September 6, and December 6) is that they allow everybody—the company, its officers, and the directors—to plan for them . Data can be made ready. Facts and forecasts can be assembled. Dates and locations can be confirmed without conflict. Remember that good directors are busy people in their own right, and to get a half-dozen influential people to convene on any given date—much less four or five dates—is a major programming problem.

Because of this need for the longest lead time possible, dates should always be set at least three meetings ahead. Don't worry, conscientious directors will see to it that they are there. That's why you pay them annually and in advance—because you want them there. You don't want to "save money" when the meetings can't be attended. If that were what you wanted, you could've saved yourself a lot of grief and money by forgetting about the whole idea in the first place.

Another good result of this commitment to fixed dates is that it puts pressure on the company management and staff to prepare themselves (and the paperwork to substantiate their arguments) well in advance. Its one thing to con The Boss, but it's pretty hard to do that to beady-eyed outsiders who expect delivery.

Meetings should be planned to last a minimum of a half day, preferably scheduled in the morning. People tend to lose their steam after a drink and a prime rib at lunch. Worse, they might dismantle the agenda by picking on parts of it for uncoordinated discussion out of sequence over the salad. Besides, it's tough for a man to be at his best at an important afternoon meeting after already having fought one war in the morning, or traveled far to get there.

Morning board meetings are also preferable because they tend to provide a reservoir of time in case something unexpected comes up and needs to be explored. With afternoon meetings, just when things start getting interesting, the directors start becoming agitated because they have to catch a plane, get home, or make a dinner party.

It's not necessary that all meetings be held at the home office. Of the four meetings per year, most should probably be held at the main office so they can include a tour to keep members up to date on the physical changes and improvements to facilities and processes. Some meetings can be held at other company locations in keeping with the need of the directors to view overall activities and management. Meetings on the business premises tend to create a serious environment for serious work. They also give the employees a chance to feel participative as they "ready up" the office for the occasion.

Unless there is a very important reason—for example, an industry meeting—resorts and other exotic locations are probably bad business, because they tend to dilute attention and confuse the issues. If you want to treat the directors to a reward for a special effort or occasion, invite the wives of all concerned and call it what it is—a chance to know and meet each other informally. It's just as deductible, and you can make an extra meeting out of it.

When the quarterly directors meetings are held, a working atmosphere should be preeminent. Minutes should be concise, to the point, and reflect accurately the ideas expressed, both pro and con. A reminder in the minutes of the spirit, as well as the substance, of the discussion and decisions is helpful to all directors in planning for future meetings.

Following advice of legal counsel, be sure you include all the necessary boilerplate and *review it.* It's the law. Don't be perfunctory.

As for the informal notes, there are some mixed opinions as to the propriety of including material over and above the legal requirements, because of potential litigation problems with the IRS and the like. You should check with your attorney. But all things being equal, a well-written record of the tenor and spirit of the discussion, distributed to the directors as soon after the meeting as possible, is a good way to keep everybody's memory cohesive.

The chairman, in addition to being prime mover and moderator, must listen. This is not just an instance of a good captive audience for his elaborate comments about his own company. His board is there to help him and get involved, not just to act as an audience.

PREPARING THE DIRECTORS

One of the most important factors to consider in making the meeting successful is the preparation of a planned, written agenda. It should be mailed to the directors as far in advance as possible. It should be accompanied by documents and materials to give the members sufficient information to enable them to make sound decisions, thus saving them from having to become speed readers at the meeting. Be careful to be both concise and considerate. Don't create such a deluge of paper that they have to ignore it altogether out of self defense.

One of the greatest problems a director faces is acquiring enough accurate information about the company to enable him to participate in intelligent discussion and make intelligent decisions. A business owner, to get his money's worth—and, more importantly, his *time's* worth—from a directors meeting , must make certain that he provides them with information which is timely and which adequately exposes them to company operations, personnel, policy, and plans.

Only the CEO and his managers can provide the board the information it needs. It's imperative to avoid situations where directors get so far behind on the operations of the company that they hesitate to make suggestions because they don't know enough. *It's imperative to avoid situations where more meeting time is spent in updates than in discussion of the future* .

Some boards seem to delight in an obsessive attention to financial statements. They get seven or eight pages of numbers, and somebody then spends two hours narrating from a prepared text. This is a waste of time. It's much better to send the statements out ahead of time, so that the directors can read them, note their questions and comments, and ask for answers either at the next meeting or through a phone call to the president if it won't wait.

The reading and commenting on every item in a quarterly balance sheet and income statement is probably the biggest of all time wasters at most board meetings. Directors who are impressed by such theatrics are not doing their job. If a "fact" can be written down, do it. Then let the directors decide what facts they want to investigate more fully.

When directors are uninformed they tend to be useless. When directors are *underinformed* , however, they have the capability to do more harm than good. While uninformed directors need to be re-educated at every meeting, and require more meeting time for informing than directing, *underinformed* directors don't know how much they don't know, and they can find themselves approving decisions and recommendations which sound good, but don't fit the facts.

The business owner should indicate what things he feels he is doing correctly both in preparing his future plans and in carrying out the recommendations from past directors meetings. There are times when this may require a great pile of papers to support the points prepared for the directors. To assist the directors in digesting the material, the Boss may want to prepare a brief outline and identify the material accompanying it as "exhibits" or "schedules."

Putting together the agenda and all the information needed to support it is the responsibility of the chairman. The absorption of this information by the directors *prior to the meeting* is crucial. Over a continuing period, it can provide them with a profile of the development of the company and may offer clues to questions which should be asked—questions which the president either may not see or is unwilling to ask himself.

A director can't fulfil his responsibility to the company and to the president if the president doesn't help him understand the company's past, its present, and his hopes for its future.

KEEPING DIRECTORS INFORMED

In addition to information prepared for the quarterly meeting, there should be periodic reports between meetings to keep board members up to date. No one can argue with or support the Boss's business decisions unless he gives them the information they need to be able to question him intelligently. Remember, it's because we want their help that the whole process is being established. Don't try to see how little help you can get. Do a good job. Again, whose benefit is all this for, anyway?

When board members are not prepared, it is usually because the president hasn't given them information. When they come to a meeting without any knowledge of what is going to be discussed, they aren't in a position to be very helpful. Worthwhile opinions cannot usually be given off the cuff, and trying to make speed readers out of directors by giving them data just as the meeting starts just isn't going to work. Moreover, good directors will come to resent it as a limitation on their ability to contribute.

Distribution of information is always a very touchy subject in closely held companies. The amount of information given out depends on how secure the owner-manager feels in his business. Actually, there is no point in his worrying about the past, it's the future he is trying to protect.

Invariably, however, those who need help the most, share their information the least. Presidents who need protection the least, share information the most. This is the nature of the species. The more inbred the company, the more fearful its owner seems to be.

Some misguided chief executives will even try deliberately to misstate the facts to their directors in order that their own actions not be questioned. This is dishonest, as well as stupid and potentially disastrous—a lot like cheating on your examination for a pilot's license. (Such dishonesty is either suicide or murder, depending on the number of people in the plane when it goes down.) If a business owner has good directors, it is a waste of everybody's time to treat them as a high-priced decoration or sterile status symbol.

In order to contribute to the well-being of any company, competent board members will demand to be kept well informed at all times of all important policy considerations. They will expect to receive accurate and timely evidence, financial and otherwise, of the overall competent performance of management, with respect to both the short and the long range goals and objectives they helped establish.

SOME MEETING RULES OF THUMB

Scheduling, organizing, and running a directors meeting are not skills most of us are born with. We don't even learn them as we build our businesses. They just don't seem natural. But they are necessary.

Every company is different, of course, but these common approaches should be useful in your own planning. To recap:

A. **Frequency.** How often the board meets is usually a function of company size. Most companies generally schedule quarterly meetings. But some larger or more rapidly changing companies can need their board's help as frequently as every other month.

Directors agree unanimously that meetings should (1) be regular and (2) be scheduled a year in advance. Competent people are very busy, and it's essential for them to be able to block out their time.

B. **Preparation.** It's essential to explain well to your directors *why* a nice guy like you wants/needs them. It should be clearly stated to each member, individually and to the board collectively, that you need all the help they can give you. Make it as explicit as you can. Like the boy said to his girl, "It's not your tacit acquiesence I need. It's your enthusiastic participation."

With *new* directors, it's good practice to send a package containing the corporate history, financial history, product lists, organization charts, biographical data on key people and the other directors, plus any other important background information,

The objective of all information is to make the new director as familiar as possible with the company. It's important, too, to meet with new directors individually before the first formal meeting and walk them through your operation and organization. A chance for them to introduce themselves at some length to the other directors can also be helpful. Biographies of directors should be made available to all company management, as well as to the other directors. Be proud of them and their commitment to you. Their election to your board should also be a "news item" in the local press, as well as in the industry media. It's notice to all that your company is planning for its future.

For every meeting the president is well-advised to send each board member, at least 2 weeks in advance, a package of detailed information. This should always include the agenda, plus up-to-date financial statements, sales forecasts, budgetary information, and operating plans, as appropriate. He should also inform them of any organizational changes that have occurred or are contemplated, as well as any changes in markets or products that are under consideration.

C. **Meetings.** In actuality, meetings can be held at your offices, your club, the lawyer's office, or in a hotel—just so long as the place is convenient, private, centrally located, and easy to reach. But, for a first choice, most owners should hold board meetings in their own offices. An advantage to this is exposing all employees to the existence and discipline of a board.

A good beginning is a short review of the previous period—what was supposed to happen, what did happen, why, and why not. Here is an excellent place for managers to present their plans, if they exist. This is a good chance to allow the directors to size up the key managers, as well as to gain understanding of what is being done and being planned. Managers should present their reports, time should be made available for questions, then the meeting should be closed to anyone but directors and specific designated guests, such as legal counsel, auditors, or other advisors.

Meeting length can vary widely. Morning starts are most popular because everybody is more likely to be fresh and because sufficient time is then available later if the need arises. Plan on a minimum of a half day and a maximum of all day. As the board "settles in," the meetings tend to expand.

The owner-manager chairs the meeting in almost every case, and guides the discussion through the prepared agenda, usually supporting his introductory comments with exhibits which expand on the material directors have already received.

Minutes are most often kept by the chairman, although some use clerical assistance. Seldom, if ever, are minutes verbatim or even comprehensive. Their purpose is (a) to make record of those actions which are required by law to be board decisions (e.g. changes in pension plans), and (b) to note any important ideas, responsibilities, and assignments for future action and review.

Four factors will effect the usefulness of agenda discussions by the board:

a) **Preparation of the directors.** The more the directors know about problems and opportunities *before* the meeting, the more likely their comments are to be valuable and to the point.

b) **The Questions Asked.** The way problems are presented and how input is sought determines the answers given. Think the problem through carefully and thoroughly. The board should evaluate reasonable alternatives, not usually suggest them.

c) **The Objectivity of the Directors.** Self-interest, conflict of interest, or lack of mutual respect among the directors can be very destructive to honest discussion.

d) **The Attitude toward Advice.** If the owner takes criticism or disagreement in an open, flexible way, the input from the directors will tend to be frank, open and valuable. There's no other way to run a board meeting.

Almost to a man, business owners who have competent outside boards swear by them. Many have been saved from major mistakes. Often, totally original and valuable ideas emerge from meetings.

All that's required is that the owner manager be willing to be constructively reviewed by competent peers who have been prepared for the questions and who accept, with enthusiasm, the responsibility and the challenges presented to them.

A director in a family company must get involved in more then just business and policy decisions, however. Part of the reason why serving on the board of a privately held company is so challenging is that it requires involvement in the whole spectrum of human life.

The board exists to ensure that the company continues, and a major part of this role may involve carrying the company through the unexpected death or disability of the owner. To do this, the director must know and be accepted by the key employees, the potential successors, and the owner's family.

Among other things, the board serves *in loco parentis*—in place of the parent—when tragedy occurs. Because the family is so important and influential in the family business, the directors must be well acquainted with the wards in their charge.

This doesn't happen by accident. It must be encouraged and cultivated.

THE FAMILY AND THE BOARD

If you have a board or are about to put one together, your planning cannot stop with selection, compensation, scheduling, and the meeting agenda. All this is important, but it's not enough. You must also go through the folloing important checklist relative to your family:

( ) *Does your spouse know, respect, and accept each director?* It's important for her to spend time with them, to know that they have you and her interests at heart. She must believe they are competent, compassionate, committed to her husbands goals/ideals, and concerned for her well being as well as for that of the business. If her husband is not able to act as he has for all these past years, will she accept, gladly and without reservation, their direction and new leadership? Or like too many widows before her in the absence of an establshed surrogate, will she fall victim to one or more of the many Rasputins whose self-interest rarely if ever coincides with the widow's, but whose emotional hold over her eventually destroys her?

( ) *Does each director know the abilities and limitations of your potential successors?* In the event of your disability or untimely demise, the board will have to choose the next president. You must give them, as early as possible, an opportunity to observe and judge your successors, both among and outside the family. If not, they, too, will be unable to make the objective judgements that, of themselves, so often create the climate of fairness that encourages acceptance of the decisions being made.

( ) *Does each director know your uninvolved children? Your partners' children and their spouses? Your grandchildren? Other important members of the business mishpocheh?* The relationships among and between generations cannot be ignored when a family is in business. No monarch ruled successfullly for long without understanding the loves and feuds among his lords and barons. Siblings have multiple interests, and so do their spouses—involved or not. Inheritor/beneficiaries of a family business have deep seated feelings of "right" versus "wrong." Directors in a family business who do not take those feelings into account and deal with them up front do not completely fulfil their obligations.

Power struggles are to be avoided at all cost. If there is any way to minimize the existence of such disastrous bloodbaths, directors are well advised to step in—or face the unpleasant consequences of their inaction.

( ) *Is your board familiar with your management team?* Although key managers might not be members of the family, their skills and commitment are essential to the success of your business. Also, they deserve to know that the board of directors of the company to which they're giving their working lives to is dedicated to the continuation of that company. You can't imagine how many sleepless nights this knowledge can prevent.

Passengers in airplanes have to feel that in the event something happened to the pilot, the plane could still fly with the copilots and take them safely to their destination. Just so must the non-family "passengers" in the business feel that *when* (not if) the management transfers from one generation to the next, the business will get them to their destination. If not, you can't really blame them for getting aboard another "plane" at the first opportunity. The concept of "This Business Shall Continue Forever" has a great emotional appeal to people who have given—or plan to give—their lives in its service. We even had a special sign made up so people would know we meant it. The existence of good directors whom they know and respect can be one of the major indications of the owners' sincere desire for continuity.

It's the responsibility of the owner-manager to set up a climate of knowledge, understanding, and trust between the board and the business family. This can be done in many ways.

Just as you have periodic board meetings, business owners should schedule periodic social events to bring this extended family and the board together. If this isn't possible, or if you feel uncomfortable with it, individual directors and key managers can be invited on appropriate occasions to your home for dinner. Directors have to eat like everyone else.

The important concern is one of continuity. Friendship and understanding are not produced by one meeting, and these meetings between the board and your family should be renewed at least a couple of times a year.

Continual attention must also be given to the relationship between the board and the successors. Perhaps the best way for potential successors to regularly show their stuff to the board is to make presentations at the regular meetings, to explain and defend their work, and their ideas. It's great experience, a good discipline, and it develops the necessary knowledge and respect.

An additional benefit of this understanding is that the board can then help owner-managers with the painful job of choosing the next president from among the extended business family.

A board of directors is installed to help ensure continuity. Unless the owner-manager opens his family doors as well as his business doors to them, however, they are forced to work at half power.

Section III

Some Commonly Asked Questions...

Chapter 7

About the Board and Our Family

The concept of using outside directors in a family-owned business is a complex one. Both the preparations and the processes are involved and lengthy. So it's only natural that new unanswered questions will be raised by the very explanations given.

Additional and usually worrysome thoughts, doubts, and objections always surface—though, too often, they're raised too late to be answered in context—and these questions, taken as a whole, often represent serious concerns about installing a working board.

The questions arise for a variety of reasons. Sometimes they're repetitive, which usually means the questioner is seeking reassurance that the answers are, indeed, acceptable. Sometimes, they're little more than a rephrasing of earlier questions that have already been answered. In all cases, though, they invariably express concerns about the contingent risks—the continuing "what if's"—that must be answered satisfactorily if we're going to have the understanding and support of the questioner.

Installing a working outside board isn't just a business decision. It has important implications for and effects upon the family/families involved in the business, and there are many important *family questions* that need answering.

In many ways, these are the most important questions. The family problems and concerns in a family-owned business are usually at the root of just about every major problem the business faces. Outside directors can fill many roles with respect to the family, and in those roles they can act as both buffers and peacemakers. They can provide that necessary "objective" viewpoint that is so necessary to preventing the increasing emotional feedback that harasses so many owner-managers and their management teams.

But this good effect of outside directors on the family doesn't happen automatically. Nor does it come about overnight. At its base, it depends on the development of trust and respect, all in an atmosphere of acceptance of the moral authority held by the outside board. Achieving this trust and respect is no easy task, particularly in a family business where the new board's job is more a curative one than a preventative one. Still, it can be accomplished. It's accomplished every day.

It's just that The Boss—the ultimate decision maker— must be convinced ("beyond a reasonable doubt," as juries are instructed) that it's a good enough idea in the first place to be worth the anguish it can cause in its creation.

There are several major areas of concern when it comes to the board's relationship to the family:

First, there are questions about getting the board accepted by everybody involved. Assuming The Boss is ready and willing to subject himself to the discipline and challenge of a working outside board, it's often very important for him to pursuade others—members of his family, his partners (if he has any), minority shareholders (if he's "blessed" with them), and his present "directors," who probably have a vested interest in remaining on the pseudo-board they presently inhabit—that a real board is a good idea. He usually has the legal "power" to form such a working board, but often his emotional and political base is not as firm as he'd like it to be.

Putting together a real board of directors, one composed of outside risk-taking peers of the owner-manager, is often one of the toughest jobs a *successful business owner* has to face.

Helping or persuading him to do so is definitely one of the toughest jobs faced by *his successors*, *his family*, and the *many others around him* who are genuinely interested in the future and well being of his business.

When they're being honest with themselves, *successors* admit that they'd like to have the Old Man hang in there so they can have his guidance over some of the rough spots. If only, they hastily add, he would be a little more articulate, less opinionated, maybe even listen more. They would like him to recognize and accept that managing the unknown changes in the next 30 years (from now well into the first quarter of the next century!) must be his successors' responsibility, and that the future is going to be much different from the well-known and now familiar changes of the last 30 years (from Pearl Harbor to OPEC!), which were The Boss's responsibility.

Mothers and widows, siblings and spouses should be comforted knowing that a real board can not only be a restraint on "The Kids," but also a source of fairness and support for their positive actions.

For his *advisors* to suggest that The Boss create a board, and then help him do it might be among the finest things that they can do for him, individually or collectively. Among all good advisors to CEO's there is always a feeling that there is so much more that they could contribute—if only the request were made of them. How mutually rewarding it would be for a good board to ask them to perform (and genuinely appreciate their performance) to the best of their technical ability, without asking them also to become enmeshed in ancillary activities that are foreign to them and their expertise.

Major suppliers of products and services could do little of greater importance for their customers (or clients, or franchisees, or distributors, or dealers) than to help support the business owner's efforts in this direction—support that can be given in the form of training, technical help, and active attempts to understand the business owner's problems. It should be apparent that the supplier's self-interest is served best if these family-owned businesses continue to survive and grow.

Minority shareholders —both within and outside the family—should welcome the willingness of the majority owners to accept the help of competent outsiders in their quest for growth and continuing profitability. It's far better than having to depend on them—the minority owners—for what everyone knows is unqualified opinion.

Managers and employees should be relieved and encouraged to see that The Boss is willing to have his "divine revelations" reviewed by those with nothing to gain. It can be the greatest assurance they'll ever get that the symbol and guardian of their economic security is dedicated to continuity.

The second major area of concern is deciding the appropriateness of various owner/shareholder/relatives serving as directors. The Boss, if he understands the concept of the outside board, doesn't have a problem with deciding. He knows that generally such directorships are inappropriate. The questions exist, instead, in the heads of the insiders who are—or want to be—on the board.

Next, there are questions that deal with the board's relationship to the family members. How close do directors need to get to the family? What are the dangers involved with doing so, if any? How can the proper relationship be set up? What are the most important concerns that must be addressed?

Why more questions?

Because every question that follows has been asked over and over again by somebody who is introduced to the idea of outside directors in the family business but still isn't totally convinced. They represent valid (and, sometimes, invalid) worries about how to proceed and survive in these uncharted waters. Without acceptable—and accepted—answers to these questions, a new board will be crippled from the start, if, indeed, it is born in the first place.

1) **How can an owner-manager be persuaded that he needs a board? Is it really such a good idea?**

Most likely he can't be persuaded, at least not directly.

This question usually comes from successors who are convinced that a board is in their best interests, as well as the best interests of Dad and the business, but don't know how to get the "stubborn old guy" to listen to "reason."

A successful business owner is unlikely (putting it mildly) to submit himself to the trauma of outside review in order to solve somebody else's problems. He isn't likely to run right out and create a board of hard-nosed, uncowed peers simply because somebody suggests it might be a good idea. It's too serious a step for that—to him, it's much the same as giving up a "happy" bachelorhood for the steady disciplines of marriage to a very serious-minded wife.

Anyone—successor, advisor, supplier, spouse, manager, or minority owner—who intends to sell a successful owner-manager on the idea of creating a working board of outside directors will have to decide, first, just what value that board will have for that particular business owner. Which of *his* problems will such a board solve? What benefits will *he* get from the existence of such a board? Why will those benefits outweigh the risks and discomfort of opening up the business "closet" to the scrutiny of outsiders?

These are the arguments that pursuade. Owner-managers don't reject the idea of outside directors because they're naturally cussed or contrary. They simply don't see the *need* . They don't see the *benefits* . They don't see any *real, practical, measurable returns to them* for having such a board. Any attempt to convince The Boss this idea is sound will have to concentrate on these aspects.

Philosophy, by itself, is not enough. Only if The Boss can be shown actual value to *him* and to his *business* , will the seed be planted in the proper soil.

2) Why should I set up a body of people who would have the power to fire me if they wanted to?

This is one of the persistent myths about the power of outside directors. Business owners often express the fear that their outside board—should they set one up—will take control of the business away from them. Maybe they'll even fire the owner-manager!

Well, it's true that a board can hire and fire the CEO. And, legally, it's possible that an outside board (or any board, for that matter) could decide to fire The Boss. A board could do that...and commit suicide at the same time.

The power of any board in an owner-managed business is a moral power only. Even though the board can hire and fire the CEO, if that "ex-CEO" happens to be the chief shareholder *he, in turn, can elect (and "de-elect") the board* .

So there's little chance that a business owner who sets up an outside board is going to find himself out on the street, stabbed in the back by the Brutus he created. It's worth considering, however, that if a board is willing to go so far as to suggest the departure of the CEO (assuming the board was properly chosen in the first place), they might have raised a good point about the continued value of his abilities as a manager to his own company.

3) **I think my sons, who work with me in the business, are convinced that outside directors are a good idea. My worry is about their wives—is it important that they agree, too?**

It's not so important that they agree as it is that they understand what is being done. In many ways, it would be a mistake to give spouses of our successors the impression they have some kind of veto power over the formation of an outside board, so to ask them to agree probably wouldn't be appropriate.

But gaining their understanding is another thing entirely. Without the understanding of our successors' spouses, we will lose one of the major benefits that come with installing outside directors on our boards.

Directors are important to successors, particularly if there are multiple successors in the same business. Outside directors can provide the necessary judgement and review to put the management transition process on an objective footing. Outside directors can help convince those involved that *competence* and *performance* are the sole criteria for promotion, not blood, sex, relative age, or the fact of marriage.

Successors need this sort of atmosphere for their own confidence and self respect, but their spouses need it, too. Remember that the business owner's daughters-in-law place their primary loyalty in their own families first. If they ever come to feel that their families are being harmed by their father-in-law, their brothers-in-law, the business, or the board, they will most likely become implacable (and powerful) foes.

A working board can help defuse this potential. It can provide a means whereby we can absorb that considerable loyalty and influence within the business and the family for the benefit of all involved. The problem is, of course, that the board cannot have this effect unless it is understood by, and familiar to the spouses of the potential successors.

There are very specific actions we should take with regard to our daughter-in-law. Instead of asking her to agree to the formation of the board, we should tell her why one is being created. She needs to hear that we want to be fair in our selection and organization of the successor management team. She needs to hear that we want the development of her husband to be measured and tracked by people who can be objective about his abilities and his weaknesses—for his sake, for the owner's sake, and for the sake of the business. She needs to know that there will be some authority in place to hold the business together in the event of The Boss's untimely departure. She sees her husband making a significant commitment. She, too, is committing herself and her future to the business. She needs to feel its future is more broadly based than the present owner's abilities.

She needs, too, to understand that there will be judgement of respective competence, that the business is, in fact, a business and not a bottomless economic cornucopia existing solely to keep her husband off the streets and her children in designer jeans. A board symbolizes the importance of competence and hard work to a fragile profitability. This understanding can, early on, defuse potential rivalry among successors' spouses over who, indeed, should be the next president/CEO.

Just as an outside board can help The Boss sleep better, just as it can ease the anxiety and frustrations of being his successor, the board can also simplify the life of our successors' spouses.

But the board won't do any good for her at all unless she knows about it and understands it.

4) **Wouldn't an outside board be seen as a threat by my key managers?**

Why would they be afraid, unless they have done, or failed to do, something an outside board wouldn't stand for? Then, too, there's really nothing wrong with a healthy dose of respect for the board's position as a judge of management performance.

There's nothing like impartial outside review to motivate a manager.

But there's something else that a board can bring to key managers, a real benefit that should be pointed out to them before the board's in place. Outside directors symbolize an opening of The Boss's mind and a willingness to listen to new ideas and other approaches, something every key manager in a family business wants very much.

5) **As a minority owner, I don't trust the intentions of the majority owner. Why shouldn't I stay on the board to see that he doesn't take advantage of me or my kids?**

If you feel (and fear) that strongly, you'd probably be better off to get out. You need a stock repurchase more than an outside board. There aren't many things worried minority owners with little faith in the management can do except harass. Life's too short for that.

6) **What possible advantage can there be in going from the quick decisiveness of a business owner to the slow, plodding decisions of a committee? What good is a "majority opinion"?**

It's probably better to ask whether there is such a thing as a majority opinion at all.

Most entrepreneurs succeed based on their own wits. They don't stop to see how many people agree with them before they go ahead, so they often feel a board will do nothing but second-guess and come up with decisions that are watered down because of the necessity for a number of people to agree.

But majority opinions are not what an owner-manager will get from an outside board. Instead, he will either get a general nod of *approval* on his decisions, from a panel of peers who essentially multiply his own judgement by the number of outsiders on his board, or he will receive a general sense of *rejection* . Outside boards of family businesses rarely "split" in their opinions on issues. Instead, they rapidly reach a consensus. It's usually The Boss who's the holdout when disagreement occurs.

Competent directors will seldom, if ever, agree totally on everything, but they understand the value of a good idea. If most of them feel—for whatever reason—that a given judgement or decision is wrong, The Boss better listen.

7) **Why is an outside board different from an inside board?**

Because, in a family-owned business, an "inside" board is really no board at all. Be honest with yourself.

8) **Three of our directors are old-timers who worked for Dad. How can I tell them to get off the board of a company they feel they helped build?**

With compassion, with love, and with respect—but it must be done, for their ultimate best interest as well as the company's. If they also have a stock interest acquired in the "old days," just hope it's restricted stock. In any event, try by all appropriate means to repurchase it. Bits of stock scattered around in uninvolved hands can cause all kinds of problems as companies pass through generations.

9) **How can I get the help I need from my accountant unless I put him on my board? It could keep him up to date and involved, not to mention that it might lower his fees.**

The AICPA (American Institute of Certified Public Accountants) frowns on members serving as directors in companies they serve. In some cases, such directorships are prohibited. The obvious conflict of interest in having directors "judge" the merits of and "validate" the effectiveness of their own work should be apparent. If only more professional advisors would recognize the wisdom of the AICPA's position and do likewise.

10) **Our present board rarely meets in any formal way. We go through the motions of making legal minutes up, but do little else. As far as I'm concerned, I already have the advice of a good attorney and a good tax consultant, so why do I really need a board?**

Many people perceive the board of directors as a group of people who serve as technical advisors to management, chosen solely on the basis of their specialized knowledge in some field, knowledge that's needed by the corporation.

So why is this any different from the job filled by professional advisors, like attorneys, accountants, bankers, financial planners, or any other consultants? If directors are nothing more than professional advisors, and we already have good advisors, then what use is a board?

The confusion here arises from a misunderstanding of the director's job.

Corporate directors have one major responsibility: assuring the continuity of the company they direct. This is a long-term objective that goes far beyond immediate management problems or technical expertise.

A director has the responsibility to seek the best possible technical advice for the corporation, of course, but he's expected then to take that advice and put it into a context where it fits well and properly with the director's major objective: the successful continuity of the business.

The best tax advice (translation: the most immediate savings in dollars), for example, may not be the best answer for the business if it doesn't fit the people or the objectives of the owners. There are many sound tax alternatives that don't assume dollar savings are the sole concern of owners. This is a judgement call, and it's best made by directors, not advisors.

As one business owner remarked, "I know I'm not going to get a better seat in Heaven just by telling St. Peter that while I was here on earth, I really shafted the IRS."

For example, generation skipping in ownership transfer may be an excellent way to avoid taxes, but transfer of ownership to grandchildren rather than children is much more than a tax matter. The survival of the corporation could be at issue, as well as the solidarity and happiness of the family.

11) **My partner and I have a buy-sell agreement. Isn't that enough to assure continuity—why do we need a board?**

Such agreements are great in the early stages of a new business, but as you get older, and some of your children become interested in working for their family business, how do you explain to them the possibility that they could become "bought out" shareholders (disinherited children) in the event their Dad dies first? Such a sword of Damocles does little to motivate either successors or long-term managers. An outside board is a far better and more flexible instrument to preserve the best interests of all concerned.

12) **From what I've seen of boards, I believe most of them are rubber stamps anyway. Usually they're run by one strong individual, the owner. The other directors on the boards I've seen rarely participate usefully in the discussions, or anything else, for that matter. They just show up at the meetings and offer their advice on the subject of the moment, in most cases lacking the background in the particular business and not having done their homework. Who needs that kind of help?**

Nobody, but that's not the kind of help available from a true working board.

Business founders are powerful people who seem to think directors are going to clutter up their lives with embarrassing or difficult questions. That's the last thing these Great American Heroes want...but also the first thing they need.

The fact that most boards are rubber stamps isn't a criticism of the concept of outside boards, it's an indictment of the owner-managers who set them up.

Presidents who surround themselves with "yes" men are not managers. They are insecure dictators who are trapped within their own opinions and methods.

13) **My attorney has been on the board since we started. How do you suggest I tell him I don't need him anymore?**

Invite him to attend the board meetings as "legal counsel" instead (making it clear that his attendance at these meetings should be included in his legal fees). His presence as such can assure that no legal requirements go untended, yet will relieve him of the non-legal risk judgements his directorship presently implies. Most likely he will appreciate the relief you are offering him.

14) **If you run your own business, as I do, you soon learn that there are times when you can make money, and then there are times when you don't make any money (because of the need, for example, to invest for expansion). Why would outside directors be willing to put up with my not making a profit?**

Sometimes profits have to be plowed back into the business to achieve necessary growth, a valid point. The complaint that directors just wouldn't be able to understand this is actually saying that outsiders can't really understand what it means to own and run a business.

This is only true for outsiders who have no experience with business ownership, either through running their own businesses or working closely with others who do.

But an outside director for a family-owned business should be a peer, a risk-taking peer, of the business owner. This kind of person *would* understand...and would be able to evaluate whether the business owner's decisions regarding profit and growth are good judgements for the future of the business. It's *your* job to find these kinds of men. You can't honestly believe your Maker only made one perfectly rational man.

Who could be in a better position to know what's needed to run a successful business than other successful business owners? If you can't explain it to them, maybe your idea isn't so great, or your facts are confused. Maybe you'd better go back and think it over.

15) **When Dad died, he left mother 55% of his stock, and 15% to each of his three children, to be held in a trust and administered by her and the bank until she dies. She's now**

chairman and she put all three of us and our spouses on the board. We meet monthly for dinner at her house. What do I do now? I'm supposed to be the CEO.

Lots of luck! Try to explain to Mother and have her understand that your desire for a real board is not a question of love or respect, or anything like that. You can, of course, always talk shop when you have dinner as a family, if that's what she wants, but our experience is that shop talk at dinner usually only leads to hard feelings (better to simply enjoy the dinner and the family). Mom must understand that *the company needs all the help it can get* . The opportunity to attract such talent to the company at the board level shouldn't be diluted by irrelevant "family" discussions among "family" directors.

16) **I've found that having just my two inside directors, who are with me at all times, lets us talk things over right away and get something done. Why would an outside board do anything other than argue about things which aren't relevant to the immediate problems of the day.**

If it is a true working board, that's exactly what it would do—and thankfully so. They're *not* supposed to act like a management committee.

The average lifespan of a family owned business is so disappointingly brief (about 24 years) because few business owners take the time to think about such questions—the questions *not* relevant to immediate problems.

Understandably, sometimes, the future may not be something the business owner wants to spend a lot of time on. In fact, in many cases, he doesn't have a lot of time to spend. Even so, he must take the time to do it—and an outside board is the most effective tool to help him accomplish his hopes for the future by making him pay attention to them.

17) **I'm a widow. If I don't sit on the board to protect my interests, how can I feel secure?**

By selecting the finest people you can to act as outside directors, by sharing your hopes and plans with them, by staying in close touch with them, and by making sure that *all the facts* they need are made available to them. Good directors would be honored by your trust in them and would work hard to deserve it.

18) **I think to expect something useful from an outside director is to expect too much. That's kidding yourself. That's the way I feel about it, and I think everybody else operates the same way I do...but they don't say it. The kind of guy you want is busy, and to really help you, he's going to have to be pretty big-hearted to take valuable time from his own business to work with you. For, say, $750 or $1000 a meeting, you have him three, maybe four times a year. How much can you really expect from him?**

In one sense, it is a lot to expect. The help we would want from an outside director is something we could never buy. A director's thought and commitment are not for sale or available at any price.

When we select directors for our businesses, that selection is an expression of respect. We are telling them that we hold their business ability in esteem, and that we trust them enough to take them into our confidence about our most valuable asset—our business.

We pay them a fee, not because we are buying their services, but because we want to acknowledge that their time and service are valuable, and that serving on our board is serious business.

Therefore, when a man or woman accepts a position on a family business board of directors, they accept this trust and they state that they are willing to fulfill the repsonsibility offered.

What we pay for can't be accurately valued in dollars. Instead, the mutual respect, support, concern, and commitment that are exchanged are as important as any payment could be.

The best of what directors offer, they offer out of challenge and respect. Maybe this *is* too much to expect from other human beings, but if we didn't expect "too much" in general, and act on those expectations, many of the things we value in life would be impossible.

19) Both of my sons and my son-in-law are with me in the business. They help me make all the decisions. Why shouldn't they be on the board?

Three heirs and potential successors, plus the CEO, on the board—added to three or four outsiders—are going to make a rather cumbersome body. If their specific responsibilities need to be discussed, invite them as a resource. The boardroom is not a schoolroom for job training. Three successors of varying talent can render meetings useless. Unless you have decided who the next CEO will be—and let everybody know—you are well advised not to make the judgement de facto by inviting just one of them. You can probably explain this to the "boys," but be prepared for some explosions among their spouses.

20) I put my company together 20 years ago, with four other men as minority owners. They are among the most respected men in town. We all sit on the board together, and we see each other often. What's wrong with that?

Nothing. At least not right now, but you should anticipate the time when the value, liquidity, and distribution of their shares are going to be more important to them than the company's future—or yours. Both successors and employees can get real nervous over *their* future in a company that's just considered as an "investment" and treated accordingly. An outside board can have the guts and wisdom to try to minimize the impact by helping find a way out of this inevitable impasse.

21) Why would minority shareholders agree to bringing strangers onto the board of a business that probably represents one of their most significant assets?

Generally, at the outset, they probably won't be willing. Also, as a matter of fact, they shouldn't be asked to accept "strangers." When it comes to an outside board, there are two issues to be settled with minority owners. First of all, they have to be shown that the board can benefit them. Secondly, they must know the directors chosen before they can accept them.

One of the most common complaints expressed by non-involved minority shareholders in family businesses is their worry that nobody is watching out for "their interests." Since they're not involved with the business on a day-to-day basis, since their interests often conflict with the interests of the managing owners, and since ignorance builds suspicion in direct proportion to the importance of the issue, minority owners tend to become distrustful and obstructive.

An outside board can relieve many of these pressures for them. The board exists in a sort of "watchdog" role with respect to the business. Its job is to keep management on its toes and to keep the business growing and profitable. This is exactly what the minority shareholders would do if only they knew how. The board also serves to balance management and shareholder conflicts in favor of the overall health of the business, something almost all parties to the situation would agree is necessary—if they could agree on the standards used in striking that balance. The board can do this, too.

In all these ways an outside board can relieve and defuse the almost natural tendency toward distrust on the part of minority owners. But this requires that these less powerful shareholders *trust the directors* . Clearly, if the outside directors are perceived as cronies of the managing owners, the ultimate effect of installing the working board will be to increase distrust and encourage conflict.

Selling the idea of a working outside board to non-involved owners must be a two-pronged process. Once they are sold on the value of such a body, they must be sold on the people chosen for that board. While they don't necessarily have to be involved in the selection process (there's a danger, here, of their feeling the directors *they* select are *their* representatives), they should have a chance to meet and get to know potential candidates and their reactions should be sought.

To fail in either of these sales jobs is to fail to get the full benefit of the outside board in encouraging harmony and cooperation among all the owners.

22) **Should shareholders agree unanimously on any outside directors who are chosen?**

It's not absolutely necessary, but if unanimous agreement can be reached, half of the board's job with the shareholders has been accomplished.

23) **What about the owner's spouse? Must she be sold, too?**

Well, if she's not sold on the idea, it ain't gonna work for long. Remember, she votes when nobody else is at the polls.

24) **Is it important for each shareholder group to be represented by at least one director?**

On the contrary, it's important for all of the shareholders to be represented by *all* the directors. A board is not intended to function as a contest among hired gladiators fighting for the interests of unseen, but specific benefactors. A board exists to assure the profitability, growth, and continuity of the entire business, which, ideally, is in the interests of everybody involved. Once we start setting up board factions, we have divided loyalties on a body which should have only one objective—the health of the company. This sort of situation will turn a business owner's intended helper into a narrow-minded obstructionist.

25) **How can I get the idea of an outside board started in my family?**

Getting them to read this book wouldn't be a bad start.

26) **Are you suggesting that a board of outside directors will be able to help a business owner overcome any difficulties he might have with his management?**

In one sense, yes. Any outside director who is qualified to hold the position will have a strong management background. What he has done and learned over the years is experience that can be brought to the aid of the business owner who is having management problems.

But recall that the job of the board is not to *manage* the company, but instead to *assure that the company is well managed*. These are two very different ideas.

Although there are a few universal "laws" of management, the operation of any single company is a highly individualistic, complex job. Then, too, the smaller that company is, the more unique and pressing are the problems.

It's not likely that an outside director will have the experience and knowledge to second-guess specific decisions made by operating managers. What he should be able to do is judge the validity of overall directions, major policy decisions, and even some specific questions of judgement, but, by and large, the outside director cannot fill the CEO/president's management role.

A board exists to provide judgement and advice to operating management, as well as an overall direction that management should follow. While this means the board will generally not get directly involved in management decision-making, they can sure do a lot to put those decisions on a more sound footing.

27) Should directors act as referrees in family fights?

Only if they want to see the fight continue and get their own noses broken in the process. Family fights shouldn't be seen as normally recurring events that have to be kept civilized. The director's job is to *stop* those fights, and *settle* the issues.

An outside director in a family business is well advised to see himself more in a rabbinical or conciliatory role than as the presiding official at an ongoing battle. If conflicts are occurring, the director should actively work to settle those conflicts as soon as possible. If he can't he should quit. Some families just want to fight.

28) Is it reasonable for women family members to expect to have women as advisors and as directors?

This question is increasingly heard as women become more interested and active in their family businesses. There is nothing unreasonable about having female advisors or directors, but there is nothing set forth in the qualifications of a director which specifies his or her ideal sex.

What *is* reasonable is expecting to have the most qualified directors and advisors possible, independent of what sex they happen to be.

29) **I'm a long-term (26 years) key employee (general sales manager). My opinions are respected by the founder. I've been on the board for 15 years, along with him, his son—who joined the company five years ago after quitting school—and the treasurer who also is The Boss's secretary. Will an outside board help me?**

Although you didn't come right out and say it, you're likely to be concerned about what would happen on the death or disability of the founder. If you're not, you should be. Such a concern is fully justified. Your company probably will have a difficult time making the management adjustments necessary to assure survival. A board like the one you describe isn't a board of directors. It's a legal fiction. Your greatest contribution to your own security as well as that of the founder and his family would be to try to convince The Boss of his need for honest advice and competent help at the director level. Perhaps you might discuss this with your professional advisors. I'm sure—if they are competent—they will have many of the same fears you have, but haven't figured out how to bring it up.

30) **Should family members be able to attend board meetings whenever they wish?**

No. They can be invited from time to time, so that they can become familiar with the board and comfortable with its decisions, but their attendance at the meetings should always be by invitation, and everybody involved should understand this. The board *must* maintain its ability to carry out its job in the best way possible. Many times this will require closed meetings.

31) **My wife doesn't contribute anything to meetings of the board, but she won't feel she's "in" on things if she's not a director. Besides, it's both an ego trip for her and it makes it more legit for me to deduct her expenses when we travel.**

Marital relations are not within the province of this book, but a man doesn't have to put his wife on the board to keep her "up to date." There are many other, better ways to do so in the course of daily life. If you want, why not invite her as a guest from time to time and have her realize how her economic security and well-being are in more capable business hands than hers. As for the "tax savings" on your wife's travel expenses, it's probable that the real value to you comes from the kick you get out of beating the IRS. Your abilities as CEO should be given more of a challenge than that.

32) **It seems to me that one of the great political values of putting in an outside board is the fact that a board can back up a business owner's plans and ideas. Is this true?**

It can be, but there are two sides to this "benefit." An outside board can have a powerful impact on the acceptability of a business owner's decisions, because the board's approval implies that objective judges have examined the decision and approve.

This support can be very useful when dealing with non-involved shareholders, successors, and key managers. The board, here, provides the protection of reasonability, where without them, decisions might appear capricious or self-serving.

But a board shouldn't be seen as a body used simply to amplify and rubber stamp the decisions made by the owner manager. It may be very comfortable to feel that we have a body of people on our side, people who are loyal and ready to go along with anything we say, but a business owner has enough of that all around him. From a board he needs—and should want—judgement and *meaningful* approval.

Perhaps the better way to state this "benefit" is to say that an outside board can be an effective way to make sure *all* relevant ideas are heard and evaluated objectively—on their individual merits.

33) How can a spouse get used to watching her husband's actions get questioned by the board?

By biting her tongue the first few times it happens, and then noting the beneficial effect such board behavior has on her husband. After this, she (and even her husband) will be likely to welcome such criticism, even though it is sometimes uncomfortable.

34) How do we go about getting unwanted directors off the board?

This depends, of course, upon who "we" are, as well as upon who the unwanted directors are. If "we" are the majority, controlling shareholders, the legal right exists to change the composition of the board. If "we" do not own the controlling interest, our only avenue is to lobby The Boss or create a majority, legally or emotionally.

The "who" in this question is important, too, because a directorship in a family business, especially an inappropriate one, is often based on relationships and ties much stronger and more subtle than simply a business arrangement.

Often, family members, other owners (or their "representatives"), long-term managers, advisors, and the like are on the board inappropriately, and we'd like to get them off. In most of these cases, simply asking for a resignation would be a very cold-hearted reward for past loyalty and service. What's faced here, again, is a sales job. These people have to be convinced that outside directors are in the best interests of the company and that their resignations are needed only for the good of the company, not because of some malfeasance or nonfeasance on their part. In most cases, once they understand, these "inappropriate" directors will agree to step down.

Obviously, some people won't be so accommodating. At times lke these, the business owner has to review his priorities and responsibilities, and act accordingly.

35) Should family guests be free to talk at meetings?

Family business board meetings are relatively informal. It's not often that the chairman imposes parliamentary procedure or Robert's Rules of Order. Each business owner must decide for himself, however, how beneficial it is to maintain an open "floor" for discussion. At all times, a sense of importance and respect for the board and its actions should be maintained.

36) Why is it so important for a board, or anybody for that matter, to provide a "court of last resort" for managers and successors?

Without question, this is one of the most beneficial functions outside directors can perform for the family-owned company, but we have always to keep in mind that an outside board has no real power in the face of opposition from the owner-manager.

The idea of a "court of last resort" implies a body of the kind of power held by, say, the United States Supreme Court, whose decisions are beyond appeal.

The board in a family company doesn't have this kind of power. It never could. An outside board can only function under the business owner's willingness to accept their judgement.

In so many senses, though, this is the only kind of environment in which a board can do anything effectively. Without the business owner's commitment, no qualified outside director would hang around very long. A board is not a "Supreme Court" so much as it is a "very influential" body. Because it symbolizes The Boss's determination to be open and reasonable, the board constantly reminds him of that determination, making it a "de facto" court of appeals.

37) What can a minority shareholder do if he or she doesn't like a board decision?

First of all, try to understand what happened. Boards usually don't make "decisions." They come to agreements, based upon the information at hand, knowledge of the company, and the collective wisdom of the directors present. If the board is properly constituted with qualified directors, its conclusions should be respected and followed. Any disagreement you have with their actions, however, be communicated to the directors. It's in their interest as well as yours that they know what the shareholders are thinking.

38) **I'm a business owner's successor, and I understand what benefit the board can be to me once I'm president. What I want to know is whether—and how—the board can help me now?**

In many ways, your outside board can be as much of a help to you now as it is to your father. Naturally, it will force you to approach the job called "successor" with a lot more attention and professionalism, but it will also clarify the standards being used to judge your ideas, as well as to measure your performance.

Disagreements inevitably arise between owner-managers and their successors. The differences in outlook, management style, and objectives are usually significant. In companies without outside directors, these disagreements are usually resolved in Dad's favor—not necessarily because he is right, but surely because he holds all the chips. If this happens often enough, *disagreements* become *conflicts* and the transition is in trouble.

A good outside board can help avoid all of this by providing an objective arbiter between the older and younger generation, weighing ideas and projects on their merits, not past history or organizational power structure. In this way, disagreements (which are usually healthy signs of an active management) will stay on the level at which they can be settled for the good of the company.

39) **How much time should a successor spend buttering up the directors?**

He should spend 100 per cent of his time doing his job the best way he knows how. If he does that, no "butter" is necessary.

40) **Why do you say that only outsiders can discuss a business owner's actions and opinions on their real merits, without self interest?**

They're not the only people who will do this, but it is definitely more *likely*, because they are outsiders, that they will. The mere fact that someone is an outsider, however, is no guarantee that they'll be aggressive with their opinions.

By looking at our needs from a new perspective, outsiders can sometimes save us from making big mistakes. Business owners must be open for the considered opinion of their directors, and actively solicit it.

This kind of open atmosphere is essential. The business owner must make it very clear to his directors, not only that he will accept disagreement and contrary opinion, but also that he *expects* their honesty and openness.

Needless to say, such advice and opinion should be had from all your paid advisors, too. There's nothing in a professional degree that says a lawyer or accountant has to keep his mouth shut, or always agree (or disagree) with his client.

Business owners have their greatest problems, however, in areas that do not fit precisely within a specifically defined area of knowledge. What we are looking for—and need so desperately to find—is the kind of effective support that's available only from someone used to wearing the same moccasins we do. Compassion and competence are not mutually exclusive.

The major value of a real, working board is not so much the *fact* of objective opinion, as it is the *kind and quality* of opinion the director can provide. Trained professionals have a very definite, and very valuable point of view, but they do not usually speak from the perspective of a fellow suffering risk taker.

This is the perspective an outside director can bring to the business owner, and the board is about the only vehicle available for getting that kind of advice in a formal and consistent manner.

**41) Will directors really choose the next CEO/president...
or will they just agree with what The Boss wants to do anyway?**

Directors will usually give their assent to the decisions reached by The Boss. But, if they've done their job, they've prompted that decision, and it was reached only after their careful consideration, their advice, and their consent. Remember that the need eventually to make this specific judgement will long have been on their minds.

Chapter 8

About Putting the Board Together

After wrestling with himself and his family until most of the human considerations, doubts, fears, and questions have been answered, The Boss faces still another set of hurdles—especially in his own mind.

Sure, he says, I *do* feel that outsiders on my board would contribute to my ultimate peace of mind, but it isn't all that simple. Where do I begin? I don't think I know anybody like that. How would I recognize someone with such qualities? What kinds of people do I need, and what would they look like?

Then, even if I get the right people, what do I do with them?

The following questions represent the most common forms these "lingering cold feet" questions and concerns take.

1) **Exactly what do you mean by a "risk-taking peer"?**

Very few of us are eager to take advice. On those few occasions where we might, it's usually from somebody we not only respect, but *who also has some "feeling" for the problem* .

Generally, the people we respect are peers of ours. They are people who generally share our way of life, people whom we respect because they have done something we respect, and people who have little reason to seek our favor. So, defining "peer" is not all that difficult.

"Risk-taking" is a little more difficult for people to understand. It doesn't refer to a gambler or wheeler-dealer. It refers to somebody who is used to the fact that his or her decisions will have significant and direct effects on themselves. The risk is in making decisions and accepting the consequences.

Business owners clearly qualify under this definition of risk-taker, but others do, too. Professional managers of public corporations can be risk-takers, and this is more and more likely to be true as they rise in the corporate hierarchy. Responsible professional managers risk their careers on every major decision they make. Some academics and some professionals can fit into this definition, too, though more rarely since their institutionalization or avoidance of risk commonly limits their compassion for those who don't—or can't—avoid it.

The reason "risk-taker" is such an important part of the definition of an outside director is the business owner's need to have his *actions*, his *decisions*, and his *needs* understood. Since his life is so involved with risk, only those who share that involvement will be able really to understand.

2) **I don't know any people like the ones you describe. How am I supposed to go about finding people with all these qualifications?**

First of all, you probably know more potential directors than you think. The problem is that you just haven't been looking at the people you know in this light.

Directors are found through an active search in our own communities and neighboring areas. They are found by asking people whom *we* know and respect to tell us who *they* respect. With this list of respected people in hand, we then have the responsibility to take the time and expend the effort to get to know these people. Every business owner has contact with some of the most competent people in his area. All he has to do is expand that contact. Wallflowers don't find directors.

Once the outside board is established, the directors, themselves, can be asked to find their own replacements—thus making a working board self-perpetuating.

3) **Why would a busy, successful person really want to serve as a director of a family company?**

This is not as difficult as it seems at first blush. There is a significant amount of honor involved in just being asked, and this naturally lessens any doubts a prospective director might have. But, also, people in business have an innate fascination for and curiosity about other people's businesses. And, too, there's a certain attraction to worrying, for once, about somebody else's problems. They, too, sometimes feel that *their* problems are overwhelming. Solving *somebody else's* would almost be relaxing—and we all think this way! Prospective directors are far from hard to convince, if you genuinely say to them "I need your help." It's difficult to turn down such a request. Would you?

4) **Is there a "best" number of directors to have?**

There are two parts to this question. First, we should decide how many directors, in total, there should be on the board. Secondly, we should decide what portion of that total should be outsiders.

As a working rule of thumb for family companies, boards with a total of five to eight members seem to work out best. While some people believe that it's necessary to have an odd number to avoid tie votes, this is really not significant for outside boards in family companies, since their decisions are not generally made by vote.

How many outsiders? The rule of thumb here is simply that they should outnumber the insiders—again, not because they should be able to outvote the insiders, but so they can feel the strength that comes with numbers. Strength encourages candid advice.

5) **So how many insiders should be on the board?**

Generally, as few as possible—just the CEO is the best arrangement. A case can be made for having owners of major portions of the stock (partners), who are also key managers of the company, on the board, but most other insiders (family or management) do not meet the qualifications needed of a director and have no real value as directors.

Their presence at board meetings should primarily be as invited guests—invited for their particular contribution.

6) **How old should a director be?**

Clearly, directors can be too young or too old, but that is seldom a problem. The key objective is balancing experience and viewpoint. One good way to look at a board is to set an "age total" which shouldn't be exceeded. This way, as the owner-manager and the existing directors get older, new directors will have to be younger to keep the sum constant. The point, of course, is to try to achieve a balance of viewpoints.

7) **How should new directors be introduced to each other?**

They should meet each other the way they would meet anybody with whom they were going to work. There's nothing especially formal about how directors are treated. They are capable, confident people who are used to—and enjoy—meeting others. It's helpful if directors know each other before the first meeting, but not critical. Taking enough time for adequate introductions at the first meeting can be sufficient. It would be unusual if they didn't have some mutual interests and acquaintances, allowing them to start working well almost from the beginning.

8) **If I go through all the trouble of finding a potential director and asking him to serve on the board, why don't I just leave him there? Why should I have limited terms?**

Tenure on a board of directors should not be forever. With time and involvement in the company, each individual director becomes less objective and less fresh. This is not to say the director's personal usefulness declines. Often, over time, a director tends to become more of a friend and less of a director. Moreover, after too much time on the board, his contribution becomes rather predictable. After this occurs, CEO's end up trying to "psych out" the particular directors, or resorting to "pork barrelling" to gain agreement.

Over time, most of us lose our freshness and objectivity in lots of ways. We should be happy to leave gracefully and with gratefulness all around for our contributions—before our usefulness has waned and it becomes painful for anybody to tell us.

Tenure varies with the circumstances, but a good time bracket is to rotate directors on a staggered basis every three to five years.

9) **Why should directors be paid so much?**

Outside directors fees in family companies are not meant to function as compensation. Qualified outsiders can't really be compensated for the immense value they bring to the company. Instead, fees paid to directors should be seen as a mutually accepted statement of respect and seriousness. People in business understand money and what it implies.

This is why fees should be openly discussed and discussed early in the owner-manager's relationship with any given director. The fee is an integral part of defining the very special relationship we are trying to achieve. It should be large enough so that both the owner-manager and the director think it is significant, and yet not so large that it borders on the appearance of "pressure." Annual directors fees ranging from $2,500 to

$10,000 are not uncommon for participation on the board of successful family-owned businesses, and probably should be reexamined every few years.

Fees should be paid quarterly, in advance (to remind them), and independent of attendance at board meetings (remember, you want their participation, not to save money because they don't show). Again, a directors fee is a statement, not compensation.

10) **Should inside directors be paid?**

No. It's part of their job. If the management wants a raise, or feels that all this work justifies more money, put it in their salaries.

11) **What about putting women on the board?**

This is a question that is asked less and less frequently these days, but it's still asked. In today's world, many business women work harder and make a greater contribution than many men. For a *family* company, board members don't have any need to function as token representatives, either of race, sex, politics, or religion. Their only job is to contribute the ideas and disciplines we need from them. Unfortunatly, in the past women were usually put on boards only because of their past or present familial relationship to investor/founders—or as a matter of inheritance. Today, women can and should be chosen for their competence, irrespective of their ownership or familial relationship.

12) **Who evaluates the performance of directors?**

This is a difficult issue, but a necessary one to address. Clearly, the board should constantly evaluate its own performance. It is usually a good idea, for example, to attach measurable objectives to strategic decisions made by the board so that it can readily be determined whether or not the objectives were met. The question to be answered is whether or not the board has had a positive influence on the company, to what extent, and how its value can be increased.

A board should do everything it can to avoid the "autopsy", the necessity to discover what happened after it's too late to correct the problem. One means for achieving this is to place continuing responsibility for various areas in specific directors' hands—either as committees or as individuals. Also, the agenda should include assessment of the board's performance, both as a body and as individuals (this latter, of course, with great care) at least once per annum. The chairman can do this, but it's much preferrable to have a rotating subcommittee of the board perform this function.

When it comes to evaluation of individual board members, it is important to maintain privacy and sensitivity. In all circumstances, personalities should be checked in the reception room.

13) **Is the director's responsibility to the shareholders, to management, or to the company?**

In the family business, a director has two roles, that of trustee and that of advisor. As a *trustee* , a director has responsibility to the shareholders for maintaining the growth and continuity of the company they own. As an *advisor* , he has responsibility to the management to help them do what is best to ensure the growth and continuity of the company. In this sense, the director's dual responsibility produces no conflict—everything he does is aimed at a single goal.

14) **Should the board's functions, duties, and responsibilities be defined in writing?**

As with any business planning, the writing of duties for a board is often as valuable in the process as in the execution. Putting assumptions and desires down on paper has a tendency to firm up those assumptions and desires in the mind of the preparer. We all know from experience that manuals seldom do more than gather dust once they're prepared, so the important consideration here is to do whatever is necessary to make sure everybody involved has a clear idea what the board is supposed to do and not do. If you feel this is best done by preparing formal written documents, then do it.

15) If, as you point out, an outside director doesn't really have any power over the business owner, what possible leverage can he have?

A director uses the motivating energy of persuasion as his "lever," and he succeeds because he works within an atmosphere of respect.

A business owner has to understand that no "director" is going to be able to "direct" him. No board is going to be able to show him what to do, because, in fact, competence cannot be taught. All any director can do is to point out problems and opportunities, while suggesting some approaches and methods for solving those problems and seizing those opportunities. In short, a good director requires a willing and competent "directee." If, in fact, he doesn't have one and if, in fact, his ideas, suggestions, and direction are ignored more often than not, the ultimate power the outside director has is to *quit* and return The Boss to the *status quo ante* he was (presumably) trying to change.

A director can, by his own example, help the business owner learn to approach the future in a positive and open way. Few experiences are more enlightening for a business owner than watching a qualified, experienced outside board wrestle with an issue and arrive at a solution. Just watching good people as they work is worth a whole library of "how to" books.

A good director can persuade the business owner that his problems are in fact worth solving, that his business and all his work have some permanent value that shouldn't be lost. This kind of influence isn't based in some power relationship. It's based in mutual respect. The very existence of outside directors should be enough to remind The Boss why he formed the board in the first place. That reminder, itself, is powerful persuasion.

A director will raise the important questions, without which no understanding is possible—but more importantly, he will raise questions which are meaningful and important to the business owner. Properly chosen and properly informed, an outside director is in the rare and useful position of understanding the owner-manager's *real* needs and concerns. Without this understanding, his suggestions and questions would be no more relevant, in The Boss's mind, than all of the other querelous and specious advice he gets from the outside world. Answers aren't useful in themselves. They must be answers to questions *we* think are important.

A director can, by his very presence, renew a business owner's respect for what he does every day. It's easy, after 10, 20 or 30 years at the helm to take your own job for granted, and once that happens, our competitive edge is lost. But, invariably, bring us face to face with another practitioner of our "art," and our attention is suddenly very much back on what we're doing. Too often, the business owner lowers his personal standards at precisely the time he needs them the most.

16) **How should a business owner conduct himself as president/chairman of the board?**

With a small dose of humility—and a large amount of appreciation.

Chapter 9

About Using a Board Effectively

Business owners aren't born to be board chairmen. In fact, the whole idea of a formal meeting of a real board of directors can be a terrifying prospect for someone who's been used to doing everything himself for many years—successfully, and without embarrassing questions or uncomfortable review. The very idea of having to stand up before a group of strangers and explain to them just what we've done, are doing, or hope to do can turn strong men to jelly.

This is probably one of the basic reasons why otherwise courageous and successful men quiver—and retreat, and refuse—

when faced with the thought of putting a real board together. They won't ever admit this fear. They don't have to. There are so many more "honorable" excuses they can use for not having real directors attending real meetings.

Similarly, few prospective directors are born to be directors. Most of these risk-taking peers of the business owner are business owners or executives themselves. For the most part they are successsful people who have gotten where they are because they know how to *manage* , not direct.

They, too, need to be told, and told honestly, why we chose them, why we need their help, and why we are going to listen to them. What are they letting themselves in for? What are they being set up for? What can they contribute? They have enough problems of their own that they can't solve to want to just walk into more of them without a good understanding of *why* .

It's important to put the fears on both sides to rest or you will end up with directors meetings that resemble the junior high dances where everybody wishes people would stop staring at them and let them go home.

The keys to getting full value from board meetings with outside directors are:

A) Directors who understand the commitment on *both* sides, and the role each is being asked to play.

B) Directors who are well-prepared,

C) A chairman/owner who has both the *desire* to encourage active discussion rather than passive observation, and who has the *ability* to give a good example to those others in the company management who will come into contact with the board members (his enthusiasm for this project will be contagious). The final key is:

D) Well-run meetings.

These requirements are clearly the responsibility of both the directors themselves and the Chairman of the Board.

Chairing a real, working board is anything but an inborn skill. It requires planning, forethought, experience, and a certain amount of *chutzpah*. It's a skill that comes with time, as does the ability to be a good and effective director.

The following questions reflect some of the common problems and concerns raised by both business owners and potential directors about the process of corporate directorship.

A. The Director's Concerns

1) **I've been asked to serve as an outside director on a family business board, and I accepted. My problem is the fact that I've never done something like this before, except serve on a hospital board. What should I be doing to get myself ready?**

There are a number of important, but not complicated, preparations every new director should make. Some are more obvious than others, but all of them are important:

a) *He should find out exactly what his director's duties should and will be.*

In fact, this should have been done *before* a directorship was accepted. The responsibility involved is not a small one, and every potential director has to ask himself if his reasons for accepting the invitation justify the time and obligation involved. He needs to understand fully what he's getting himself into.

There are some books and articles written on the subject, although most of them center around directorships in public corporations. Your attorney would also have this information. These can give a prospective director a sense of the legal, "boilerplate" duties and decisions usually reserved to directors, but there's much more to a family business directorship than boilerplate.

Characteristic of most family-owned businesses is the concept of *secrecy*. For a long time, many presumably successful business owners have been able to make a fetish of obscuring data, confusing the advisors, keeping the management uninformed and the family docile. Records grow harder and harder to come by, facts differ depending on the source, and most everybody involved is apprehensive over the affect of anything new on their well-being. Directors have to recognize this as a fact of life with which they have to deal and, ideally, change.

Directors have to deal with managements that have been kept in the dark and families that often have valid differences in perspective—dependent both upon their ownership involvement and the degree to which they feel insecure. These unique aspects require that the new director do some further digging.

b) *He should learn as much as he can about the company and the people involved.*

Part of the reason why this is important is the director's need to understand his potential liability. While the liability faced by family business directors is generally minimal, there are situations where it can be significant. More important, though, is the need to understand the "power" and "knowledge" structures behind the business, because both the potential and the problems of any family business depend greatly on the nature of these two structures.

It's one thing, for example, to become a director of a family company in which all relationships and operations are running smoothly, where everybody is happy—where The Boss owns 100% of the stock, where a competent management is in place, and all operations are profitable. It is another thing entirely to walk into a situation (a) where ownership is split among partners or families who don't get along, or (b) where the uninvolved minority owners have been complaining for years about salaries, benefits, expenses, and dividends, or (c) where no one but The Boss knows the whole story or where to find it.

There are a few situations—they are rare, but they exist—at which a potential director will look very carefully and then decide that the risks and the headaches—apart from any possibilities of a lawsuit—are so great that it just doesn't seem to be worth getting involved. This can't be discovered by a surface examination, though.

We would advise that any prospective director of a family-owned business meet with and listen to the significant shareholders and top managers. These are the key people within that family business. They are the people with whom he will have to work, and for whom, in fact, he does his work. Their acceptance of him (and vice versa) is paramount, but, equally essential, is his belief that he can make a positive contribution.

A prospective director must seek this understanding actively. Find out where they are located, and what they are like. What do the shareholders and managers know about the company? Are they content, or is there a family dispute brewing? Has there been a split? Are family members/owners demanding more dividends? Are they dissatisfied with management, and vice versa? What are the owners' expectations for themselves and their children? What do the key managers think about this? Is it affecting them? How?

Even further, the prospective director should obtain basic information about the *business*. He should know something about the people who run it and the competition, about the company's history and the prospects, and whether the company is progressing or slipping.

He should take a look at their financial statements for the past few years. When were they last examined by Internal Revenue? What was the result? He should ask if he can talk to their banker. A great deal can be learned from other advisors and even past directors, for that matter.

A potential director should also know why the others involved think he's been invited to be a director. What particular bias, knowledge or experience of his are they interested in? He should have a good understanding of why he's being asked to serve, and he should be convinced he really has something to contribute.

c) *He should identify any potential problems and decide if he can (and wants to) live with them.*

It's important to identify and understand the points of view of all the shareholders. There are bound to be some differences of opinion, and only when they're understood can a prospective director make an intelligent decision.

Often there are reasons to get involved in spite of apparent conflicts—out of respect for the owner-manager and his commitment to professionalism, for one example, and out of the challenge being offered, for another. In these cases the potential director should consider meeting with the dissident groups or their representatives, tell them he has been invited to be a director, and outline his qualifications and his intentions.

They should know that before he reaches a decision as to whether or not to accept the invitation, he wants to hear their points of view and to answer any questions they may have.

He may find that although they disagree, they are basically objective and reasonable, and they may have a valid point of view. If he is to serve as an outside director, they must be comfortable with him, and he with them. Again, he is not an advocate. He is *their* director as well.

In summary, an outside director of a family company is a risk-taking peer of the owner manager, who agrees to serve on this important body out of respect for the owner, out of belief in the importance of business continuity, and out of his own interest in the problems and challenges of the particular business.

2) I've been told by some people that a man would have to be insane to accept a directorship in a family company. They say that the risk of being sued is too great to make it worthwhile. Is this true?

In most cases, an individual who wants to perform the valuable function of an outside director can, after taking a few precautions, rest rather easily on the liability question, devoting his thoughts and energy to the real problems facing the business he directs.

Anyone who accepts a corporate directorship accepts an important responsibility. A directorship should not be entered into solely because of the title, honor, fee, or prestige involved.

A corporate director has a fiduciary responsibility to both the corporation and its owners, the shareholders. What potential liability he faces would arise from his failure to perform his duties *responsibly* .

A director's potential liability (assuming he's not associating with people intent on committing fraud) is only to one group of people: the *shareholders* . In a family company the number of these potential "plaintiffs" is very limited, often to one or two people. Then, too, shareholders who are active in the business are not helpless bystanders and cannot reasonably claim ignorance or disagreement with their own actions.

In rare circumstances, such as misappropriation of assets, *creditors* may have a claim against a director, but those circumstances usually involve fraud. Fraud is something a person doesn't commit by accident, so the only potential director who should worry about his potential liability for fraud is a potential director who is, himself, a fraud and associates with frauds.

Most problems, if they arise, will arise from inactive shareholders. Even these problems can be minimized, however, through reasonable care and prudence.

3) **Specifically, what sorts of actions can get me into trouble as a director?**

There are a few *overt* acts that could lead to liability. For example, if the corporation were insolvent and the assets were being improperly diverted for the benefit of the family at the expense of the creditors, the director could face some liability to those creditors. Inducing a breach of contract could lead to liability. But these are, generally, conscious, deliberate acts and, therefore, easily avoidable.

Instead, it's usually the outside director's *failure* to perform the director's duties that will cause whatever trouble he's most likely to get into. To most prospective directors, the possibility of an accusation of *negligence* is probably the most scary potential liability.

A few common examples of this "negligence" would include failure to review financial statements, failure to attend meetings, and failure to inquire about suspicious activities. Other examples might be:

Bribery . If a director learns that the corporation is engaged in bribery, but he closes his eyes, there is a potential for liability.

Illegal Payments/Loans . If a director knows the business is not legally permitted to pay a dividend, possibly due to a state law or a negative covenant in a loan agreement, and yet allows such payments, he is potentially liable. The same is true about *knowingly* permitting illegal loans to officers, or hiring a convicted embezzler to serve as treasurer.

Stock Purchases . If the corporation is prohibited by law or its own articles of incorporation from purchasing its own shares, and the director knowingly allows it, he has potentially violated his fiduciary duty.

And so on...

Most situations which lead to liability for directors in family businesses involve some form of negligence, but *negligence can be avoided by using common sense, taking the directorship seriously, and taking the time to learn the really important facts about the business* .

A director does not have to be an expert. He does not have to be an accountant or conduct audits. He does not have to be a lawyer or be familiar with all applicable laws.

But a director should take the time to understand the corporation and its activities, to attend meetings, read the statements, and question the officers. He should use the judgement we would expect from a prudent person. He shouldn't accept a directorship unless he is prepared to take some serious interest in the business.

For example, if he were invited to become a director and accepted, but no meetings were being called, he would have an obligation to ask why. This is the sort of thing that happened in a well-known bankruptcy case of a public company. The directors were sued after the company filed bankruptcy because it appeared they had not been getting the reports required, or reading the ones they got. It appeared that the officers weren't fully disclosing, and the directors weren't paying much attention. They weren't taking sufficient responsibility.

Every position of responsibility involves some exposure, but in a family company the exposure is generally minimal. Prudence and common sense and the fine quality of the people involved are the best protections against what little risk there is. With them, a director can confidently go ahead and deal with the positive aspects of the experience, benefits which far outweigh any potential for liability. If in doubt, consult your own attorney. If *still* in doubt, don't accept the offer of a directorship. It's that simple.

4) **What about liability insurance? Should the corporation provide this kind of protection to its directors?**

Many states—but not all—specifically authorize a corporation to indemnify a director for expenses and legal costs. In some circumstances—when he can establish he was not negligent—he can also be indemnified for any settlement costs.

But the state law which authorizes these corporations to indemnify directors does not *compel* them to do so. Thus a provision in the company's code of regulations providing that the corporation will indemnify the directors under specific circumstances is a good way to give further assurance to an outside director.

There are, of course, various forms of directors and officers liability insurance. It comes in all shapes and forms with deductibles, with umbrellas, etc., and a good casualty agent should be able to fill you in about the applicability of such insurance in your state. Still, given the generally limited nature of the liability problem, insurance might prove to be an entirely unwarranted and unnecessary expense. If you want to, check with corporate counsel to make sure.

5) **If I accept a position as a corporate director, how much information about the company and the owner himself should I be able to ask for and expect?**

Everything you feel is appropriate to ask should be answered.

The business owner who invites you to help him as a working outside director is making a commitment, as well as a very conscious decision to share his problems with you. In this sort of relationship, any and all information which has an impact on the owner-manager's business and financial planning should be made available to the directors.

Directors don't necessarily need to know everything there is to know about the business owner's personal financial status. Certain information might be highly intimate and have only minimal importance to overall corporate strategy, and The Boss would be justified in withholding such information from his directors. If they'd had any sensitivity, the directors probably wouldn't have asked.

Still, such circumstances are relatively rare, and the business owner who gets the most value from his outside board will generally be the one who is most open with that board about his personal and business status and plans. If a director starts getting the feeling, however, that the business owner is withholding important information, and not playing it straight with his board, that director can usually safely assume that that particular owner-manager doesn't really want a working board, and ought to quit.

Directors should, at all times, try to ask intelligent, direct, honest questions which aren't tempered by political considerations, a desire to go easy on The Boss, or fear of disapproval. Directors should approach their jobs with a conviction that they were given the right to know, and that it's their duty to question assumptions they don't understand, and to seek information they feel they must have to do their job.

Most important, they should make the assumption that The Boss wants them to understand.

B. The Chairman's Concerns

6) **I understand that directors have to have some information prior to each meeting, but is there anything special they should get prior to the first meeting?**

The major difference between the first board meeting and all the ones that follow is the need, before that first meeting, to bring the directors up to date on the history, organization, and growth of the company. Also, each new director must, at the outset, become as knowledgeable about his fellow directors as possible.

Probably the most direct approach to this updating is the preparation of a "directors manual," a detailed book of information sent to each director both for reading and for future reference. The contents of the "manual" will vary widely, depending on the nature of the company involved, but, in general, it should include information like:

a) *History and development of the company.*

Every organization is shaped and given its "character" by how it developed, and without an understanding of that history, any understanding of that organization is necessarily limited. This is particularly true of a family business, where history has a *great* influence on the present organization. Many of The Boss's opinions and prejudices are based on the experiences he had while building the company.

Knowledge of what's gone before is also important to the board for making policy decisions. History is a teacher as much as a determinant, and the board should have the benefit of learning from the mistakes and successes of the past.

b) *Ownership history (a "geneology" of the shares, so to speak).*

The history of stock distribution is a fascinating study in and of itself, but it also is critical to gaining a full understanding of any given family business. It makes a difference whether shares were "founded, " "inherited," or "acquired." How the shares were divided has a lot to do with how shareholders presently get along. Lines of descent will disclose future lines of descent—and who probably will own how much stock in the future. This information is essential to the directors.

c) *Sales, product, and competitive history.*

Directors should have an understanding of sales growth and product mix. They also need to have a sense of where specific products and services are in their "life cycles." Decisions will have to be made about new or existing products or services, overall marketing strategy, and growth requirements which can only make sense in context with the past. This section of the manual will be referred to often.

d) *Organization chart.*

It may seem obvious that the directors should have an organization chart to work from, but very few family companies *have* one available to send. In addition to the obvious informational benefit to the directors, an organization chart (or at least the drawing of one) can have a real educational effect on the owner-manager too.

e) *Biographies of key managers.*

As directors go through their manuals they will be learning what they can about the business, and they will be formulating questions and possibilities. Whatever is to be done or recommended by the board will depend a great deal upon the key managers presently in the business. Directors should have the advantage of knowing as much as possible about these people before they meet them. Salary histories and significant responsibilities/accomplishments with the company should be listed in their resumes, as well as data on personal, educational, and prior business experience.

It's a good idea to include a "bio" on each director as well, to help introduce each of them to their colleagues on the board.

f) *Comparative financials (at least 5 years back).*

The "comparative" aspect here is important. How has the company done year to year, and in what direction have the changes happened? This is the best way to help directors recognize and understand the importance of changes or variances that will come up in the future.

g) *Budgets and projections of all kinds (product, market, organizational, financial, etc.).*

These, finally, are the "stuff" of strategy. They represent both the basis for the existing control systems and the plans for the future, and provide a springboard from which the board can begin discussion of their most important responsibility— planning for the future.

ORGANIZATION CHART
AS OF _____ (DATE).

COMPANY NAME AND ADDRESS:

TOTAL NO. EMPLOYEES:_____ ANNUAL $ VOLUME: $ _____

STOCKHOLDERS:
NAME	RELATIONSHIP	%	HOW/WHEN ACQUIRED	AGE	EVENTUAL DISPOSITION
1.					?
2.					
3.					
etc.					

(§ DON'T FORGET TO INCLUDE ALL TRUSTS AND TRUSTEES.)

DIRECTORS:
NAME/TITLE	YEARS WITH CO.	AGE	TENURE	NAME/TITLE	YEARS WITH CO.	AGE	TENURE
1. /CHAIRMAN				4.			
2.				5.			
3.				etc.			

FREQ OF MTG:_____ /ANNUM   COMPENSATION: $ _____ /ANNUM

PRESIDENT
ᴮᵘᵗWHO IS THE REAL CHIEF EXECUTIVE OFFICER?
PRESIDENT?   CHAIRMAN?   OTHER?
OR MUST EVERYTHING BE A "COMMITTEE" DECISION?

ADVISORS:
NAME	YEARS WITH CO.	AGE	FREQ. OF MEETINGS
1.			
2.			
3.			

ADVISORS:
NAME	YEARS WITH CO.	AGE	FREQ. OF MEETINGS
4.			
5.			
6.			

(SO FAR YOU'VE PROBABLY GOT THE SAME NAMES IN EVERY BOX!)

NOW - FINALLY
THE MANAGEMENT TEAM!
(WHO HOPEFULLY DO THE WORK!)

—SEE ACROSS ⟶

PRESIDENT

WHAT HAS HE LEARNED? | YEARS WITH COMPANY | AGE | YEARS IN THIS JOB | WHAT HAS HE ACCOMPLISHED?

FAMILY RELATIONSHIP
(UNCLE? BROTHER? DAD? MOTHER?)

STOCK OWNERSHIP %
(COMMON? PREFERRED? HOW ACQUIRED?)

IS THERE AN EXECUTIVE V.P. OR AN EXECUTIVE COMMITTEE?

TITLE	TITLE	TITLE	TITLE
NAME	NAME	NAME	NAME
? { YRS. CO. / AGE / YRS. JOB } ?	{ YRS. CO. / AGE / YRS. JOB } ?	{ YRS. CO. / AGE / YRS. JOB } ?	{ YRS. CO. / AGE / YRS. JOB } ?
RELATIONSHIP	RELATIONSHIP	RELATIONSHIP	RELATIONSHIP
STOCK %	STOCK %	STOCK %	STOCK %

FILL IN AS NECESSARY →

AND DON'T FORGET TO PUT IN:

*<u>ALL</u> THE VICE-PRESIDENTS – NO MATTER HOW "HONORARY"

*THE TREASURER - THE OUTSIDE ACC'T? THE LITTLE OLD LADY? YOU?

*THE SECRETARY – OFTEN RASPUTIN, BUT USUALLY A WAY OF SPREADING MEANINGLESS TITLES AMONG THE FAMILY MEMBERS.

*<u>ALL</u> MANAGERS / DEPARTMENT HEADS

*<u>ALL</u> RELATIVES & INVESTORS <u>ON THE PAYROLL</u>
(EVEN THOSE WITHOUT REAL JOBS! : SUCH AS GRANDMA, YOUR WIFE'S UNCLE, NIECES FROM THE OTHER FAMILY,.. THE DENTIST? .... JUST BECAUSE <u>YOU</u> FORGET, THEY DON'T!)

AND THEN PREPARE :

*A REAL JOB DESCRIPTION FOR EVERY JOB

AND

*AN HONEST RESUMÉ
*A SALARY HISTORY
*MAYBE EVEN AN EVALUATION OF POTENTIAL!

FOR <u>EVERY</u> MANAGEMENT JOB AND JOB HOLDER.

JUST WRITING ALL THIS DOWN HELPS CLEAR OUT SOME OF THE CONFUSION.

Once directors have been brought up to date, the objective should be to keep them as current as possible, consistent with their time limits, and limits on their capacity to absorb detail.

Periodic director updates are essential, at least quarterly, and these should contain such items of current information as financial statements, projections, market and product forecasts, sales information, and reports by key managers on any topics assigned to them by the board. It is particularly important that such information—as current as possible—be sent prior to each board meeting to avoid the need for "speed reading" during the meeting itself. Only prepared directors are fully participative.

7) **What should be contained in the agenda for a directors meeting?**

The agenda will vary greatly depending on the company, the people involved, and the problems to be faced. Generally, however, the agenda should contain:

*A roster of expected directors and guests.

*Scheduled starting/adjournment times.

*Provision for discussion/approval of past meeting minutes.

*Provision for discussion of old business (which was "new business" at the last meeting).

*A listing of new business to be discussed (such items as management reports—and by whom, decisions to be reached, discussions needed, etc.).

*The schedule of upcoming meetings.

While setting the agenda is generally the responsibility of the chairman, it's a good idea, particularly as the board becomes "seasoned," to caucus the board prior to setting the agenda to make sure that subjects *they* want to discuss are included.

8) **How much information about the company should be given to the board?**

The board should know everything necessary to fully understand the company, its managers, the family, and the ownership's goals for the future. Generally, this means that nothing of this nature should be denied the board if it desires to know.

One caution is appropriate, though. The capacity of directors to absorb information is no greater than that of any mere mortal, so, while all information should be made available, it's not productive to provide them with so much that it overwhelms them. One good way to judge this is to assume no more than one hour of preparation for every hour of meeting. Use the agenda as a guide, and submit material that will make the directors' discussion of those subjects meaningful and not repetitious.

9) **How do we make sure directors do their homework?**

By doing ours and by providing them with concise, digestible, meaningful information on a timely basis. Don't smile. That's a huge job for management to carry out, and although it sounds like common sense it's seldom done properly.

10) **Should a board meeting be a brainstorming session, or carefully limited to defined subjects?**

Board meetings can serve both functions, but in all cases they should be planned and carefully controlled. The most valuable "brainstorming" comes from disciplined, prepared minds in situations where the subject being discussed is carefully defined.

The job of chairman is partially one of disciplinarian. It's his duty to guide discussion along lines predefined by the agenda—but, and this is an important "but," he should also be sensitive to and ready for totally unexpected ideas and lines of discussion which are valuable in themselves. These unplanned flashes of insight are among the extra benefits of a good outside board. Often, they are important enough to lead to *major* changes—profitable changes—in the way a company does business.

These insights don't happen by chance, however. They happen by preparation, forethought, prior experience, and understanding. The more comfortable a board gets with the company and its duties, the more their special insights are likely to happen.

And when these significant insights occur, they're usually recognized immediately by everybody. It's often as though somebody just turned on an extra light in the room.

11) **Is the first board meeting different from the rest?**

Yes, but mainly in the sense that it will be more concerned with what is expected of the board, as well as an overview of company practices, policies, and personnel, than it will be with the future operations or the future of the company. A rather significant amount of time may also be consumed the first time around in filling in omissions or clarifying ambiguities in materials submitted in the directors "manual." There will probably also be detailed questions on specific accounting terminology and reporting methods, and these questions are usually necessary to assure proper understanding.

There's a certain amount of discomfort and shyness involved with the first of anything, and boards are no exception. Remember that neither the directors nor the "directees" are professionals. The first real board meeting in a family company is usually the first real board meeting for most everybody involved. It can't be rushed, nor should it be allowed to deteriorate into a permanent convocation of business "wallflowers."

In many senses, of course, no two meetings are alike, but boards, like wine and business owners, tend to get better with age.

12) **How much should invited advisors—i.e. the attorney, accountant, banker, etc.—participate in a board meeting?**

As much, and only at such times, as the directors want them to. Board time is very limited and attendance/participation of advisors at meetings is not always necessary. Advisors participate to help the owner-manager and his directors, not to promote their special skills, contribution, or bias—and certainly not to "take over" the meetings.

It's important to note, however, that advisors tend to put in their best performances during appearances before working boards—all the more so when they are appearing in consort with other advisors. Outside directors tend to inspire professionals to do their best thinking because they meet in an atmosphere of interest and acceptance. An attorney or an accountant—any advisor, in fact—will be encouraged to be creative and thorough because he will feel his recommendations will be heard and acted upon.

Often, for the experienced advisor to a business owner, this is a totally new and welcome experience.

13) **How long and how often should a board meeting be?**

When Will Rogers was asked how long a man's legs should be, he answered, "Long enough to reach the ground." The same is true with board meetings. To be specific, though, while half-day meetings aren't usually enough to do what is necessary, meetings lasting longer than eight hours or so are more the exception than a rule. With practice, the meetings become better organized, and more gets done in less time.

Meeting frequency can be varied from twice a year to six times or more a year. This means total annual meeting time will vary from as little as two mornings (eight hours) per year (which not only won't accomplish anything, but would also lead to the question whether you really want a board—after all, you're not using it), to as much as six full days (or 48 hours) per year. This 48-hour figure seems to be pushing outsiders a bit much for their contribution, and should make you wonder if you're not actually abusing a board as an operating committee.

14) **What are the general duties of the chairman?**

The Chairman of the Board in a family company is usually The Boss. There are few specific duties connected, by definition, with this additional hat, but the chairman should do at least two things. He should determine the issues to be covered at the meeting, and make sure the board sticks to them as far as possible. Again, he must also be sensitive to the unexpected, and ready to take advantage of the considerable expertise and knowledge represented by the people at the table in front of him.

And, because he's usually also the boss, he should make sure he grins and bears the sometimes difficult or embarrassing discussions with grace and humility. They're good for him—if he listens.

15) **Should meetings be formal or informal?**

They can be either, whichever is more comfortable. Because of the nature of the relationship between an owner-manager and his directors, meetings of boards of family companies tend toward the informal. This doesn't mean sloppy, however. A certain amount of decorum and "ceremony" tend to give a certain amount of dignity to the proceedings they surround, and, with them, everybody tends to take what they're doing more seriously.

16) **Are reports/summaries of board meetings necessary?**

Yes. These "minutes" serve three basic functions. First of all, there is a legal requirement that certain decisions be made by the board of directors, and these decisions must be recorded in the minutes. Secondly, there are specific actions of the board which should be recorded to substantiate certain tax and legal strategies (your attorney is your best guide in these matters). In addition, however, the minutes provide an ongoing record of the board's advisory activity and the performance of management in listening to and carrying out that advice.

We all face the problem of overprogramming. Without a good set of minutes, even the most exciting and useful meeting of the board will decline in impact with time as everybody forgets what happened and what was said.

You might want to keep your records in two catagories. One would be the formal minutes containing the necessary legal and tax information. The other could be informal minutes, a record of the discussions and suggestions which involve some follow-up on the part of management. Over time, these informal notes will make up a fascinating history of corporate policy making. Competent counsel can help you decide what is appropriate.

17) **Is it good practice to question the president's policies and decisions in the presence of other managers and advisors at meetings?**

Within reason, it's an excellent practice. What better way is there to demonstrate to all concerned the moral authority of the board, as well as The Boss's willingness to take it seriously? Lacking this example, the tendency can be to simply write the board off as just another ego trip by The Boss.

18) **How do we avoid rubber stamp boards?**

By installing risk taking peers as outside directors, by making them a majority on the board, and by showing them you are willing to accept—and act on—their advice. This puts the burden on them to be worthy of your trust...and on The Boss to be worthy of their efforts.

Some Final Thoughts

You've stayed with us for a lot of pages. You've been asked to think about many things and to accept ideas which often seemed to go against your common sense. You've been asked to open yourself up to an experience you probably would have rejected out of hand just a short time ago. It's possible that you still believe an outside board isn't for you. You may still be struggling with some serious reservations and significant doubts.

While in some few cases an outside board is probably not appropriate, we've seen over and over again that business owners too often reject the idea of installing outside directors for the wrong reasons.

Most business owners will automatically reject the idea when it's first suggested, so strong is their desire for autonomy and "flexibility." They only change their minds when they come to reconsider the assumed value of their accustomed and beloved freedom from review.

We have asked you to reconsider these—and other— assumptions about the real advantages of owning a successful business, yet our hard-won assumptions don't dissipate overnight. We build them into our personalities, into our thought processes, into our management styles, and into our business organizations. The world we build around ourselves, and the people we choose to inhabit that world with us, reflect the way we think. To change the way we think means we have to change the world we've built. And *that* is a most intimidating prospect.

Those of us who own successful family businesses are now standing on the threshhold of the Eighties, facing a world unlike anything that has gone before. We are facing a time of limited resources, of economic regrouping, of barriers to growth. We are facing some fundamental restructuring of our society and the ways it does business. We are facing massive changes in the marketplace, most significantly an increasing demand for quality and service at a time when both competition and price sensitivity have increased dramatically. We've already lost most of the economic fat that was gained over the past 30 years, and those of us who've survived that process are being forced to prepare to run yet another obstacle course.

These changes aren't necessarily all negative. In fact, most successful business owners have confidence in the strength and potential of the future. Without such optimism, they would never have been able to build their companies under the ceaseless crossfire they've already faced.

But times are different from what they were, and they will quickly become different from what they are. Change has always been a fact of life, but today it is supercharged by the pace of events, by exploding technology, by instant communication, and by an increasing capability and consciousness among the world's peoples.

This is the world the family-owned business will inhabit in the Eighties, a world increasingly characterized by growing interdependence, interrelated responsibilities, and an ever more obvious need for cooperation and accommodation among those involved. These needs have always existed *within* the family business. The difference today is that the boundary between the closely held business and the outside world is being torn down by events, and, because of this, the parochialism and tunnel vision so characteristic of family companies is growing ever more inappropriate—and dangerous.

One simple fact is becoming increasingly clear: *No business will long survive if it does not (1) learn to open itself up to the awesome changes occuring in our world, (2) come to understand those changes, and (3) learn to use those changes to its advantage* .

Simple market/product research is not enough. More is changing than just our markets or our products. Business education is not enough. Business itself is changing. The economy is changing. People and their perceptions are changing. There is much more going on—and much more will be going on—than any one or two, or any few of us can understand alone, and yet the temptation within the privately held company is always to depend on *internal* experience and *internal* judgements.

This is the Achilles' heel of the family-owned and managed business. This is why a board of outside directors is essential to our survival and growth. This is why second-best efforts or compromise solutions just aren't going to work for long.

The family-owned businesses which will survive and grow over the next few decades will be those businesses whose owners decide, today, actively, to resist the strong tendency toward parochialism. And the best way to avoid this managerial incest in the family company is by creating and using a working board of qualified outside directors .

This openness will not come about simply because of the added knowledge that the outside directors can bring—although that will be significant. It will come about because only outside directors are able effectively to guarantee that a company will remain open to the outside world. Only a formal outside board has the *moral authority* necessary to keep the family managers open to, and actively seeking, outside information.

Outside directors represent a commitment to an ideal. They symbolize the acceptance of a significant truth: that the truly "closed" corporation cannot long survive in today's world. Because outside directors represent this belief—this commitment—only they can serve, constantly, to remind the owner-manager, his family, his successors, and his key managers why the board was formed in the first place. They will remind them of the decision that their own counsel is not enough, that they need the active help, advice, and review of others.

Even the best professional advisors will generally fail to provide this "reminder." Most so-called "advisory boards," which are really made up of "mistress directors," will fail, too, because they were formed out of a lack of total commitment to the ideal of openness.

They are all helpful. They do bring something of value to the business owner. But only a true outside board can ensure a continuity of outside help for a family business. It is far too tempting to retreat from criticism and review to leave the future to the vagaries of our own will power and to the limitations of our own knowledge.

People in advisory roles only, do not usually have strong commitments to us. It's too easy, over time, simply to stop using them, to stop seeking their input—especially if that input becomes more and more contrary to our way of doing things. And that temptation is there. It will always be there. It will always increase.

Many positive reasons for creating a working board have been presented in this book. They are all valid. But it's the board's ability to fill our need for *continued review and help* that truly separates boards of working directors from all other solutions and suggestions.

We know the thought of forming a formal, outside board can be uncomfortable, even intimidating. But we would hope, by now, that the concept of such a board has, at last, become a possibililty, and a *comforting* one at that, for your business.

For the successful family business, outside *directors* are keys to the future.

Appendix

A Director's Checklist

1) Questions about the business.

a) How well do I understand what makes this business successful?

b) How well do I understand its products? Its markets? Its money? Its organization? Its leadership? Its momentum?

c) What are its significant weaknesses? Short term? Long term? Can I help overcome them?

d) Am I willing to put forth the effort required to be a factor, as a director, in its continuing success?

2) Questions about the Priorities and Pressures on the Business Owner.

a) What are the specific characteristics which make his company different?

b) What is the ownership's true motivation?

c) What are the interactions between the company structure and the family structure?

c) What kind of imprints do they leave?

e) How do key employees respond to them?

f) How do the present owner(s) respond to them?

3) Questions about Personal and Corporate Goals.

a) Does the owner differentiate between personal and company goals? If so, how?

b) Are these goals and objectives achievable? How are they determined? By whom?

c) How can these goals be effectively reviewed, evaluated, enlarged, and updated?

4) Questions about Both Family and Non-Family Personnel.

a) How will/should I deal with multiple heirs, spouses, and other relatives?

b) How do their pressures affect the motivation and development of key managers? Of each other?

c) How do they affect the operation of the company?

d) Does the company offer realistic advancement for both family and non-family personnel?

5) Questions about the Role of Wives, Mothers, Sisters, and other Women in the Family Business.

a) What influences do these women have? Positive? Negative? Are they informed or uninformed?

b) Can they help resolve some of the pressures which are unique to this family-owned company? Do they want to? Can they work in harmony?

c) Are there any working wives? Who are their spouses?

i) What are their responsibilities?

ii) What are their capabilities?

iii) What are their goals?

d) What and how do the women involved know about their estate plans? About the financial plans of the company?

e) What are their needs in any retirement planning?

f) How well do they understand the needs of the company? Its managers? Advisors? Directors? What can be done to increase their understanding and endorsement?

6) Questions about the Owner as a Manager of People.

a) Is there full commitment from key employees?

b) Is the management team staffed to maximize the talents and abilities of its members?

c) Are the employees self-motivated to achieve their maximum productivity?

7) Questions about Outside Advisors.

a) Do competent advisors offer needed review and timely advice for the professional fees paid?

b) Is there conflict among the advisors?

c) Can they work together when necessary?

d) Has the company outgrown its advisors?

8) Questions about Succession and Continuity.

a) How is management continuity being handled in this company?

b) How will authority be transferred from older to younger executives?

c) How can the experience of the older and the talent of the younger be combined to provide the best benefit for the company? For the people in it?

d) Can successors from outside the family be installed?

e) Are the successors identified? Announced?

f) Have they proven their ability to lead?

g) What will be the pressures on older executives when control changes?

h) When and how do the present owners/managers retire?

i) Who will decide?

9) Questions about Me.

a) Am I qualified

b) Am I committed?

c) Am I motivated?

d) Am I accepted by those involved?

Index

Books about Family Business
From The Center for Family Business

"INSIDE THE FAMILY BUSINESS" by Léon A. Danco, Ph.D.

. . .the nation's recognized authority on privately held business draws on two decades of experience "inside" thousands of successful family-owned companies to write about the real keys to success: the attitudes, experiences, and relationships among the most important people in any family company...**the family members themselves.** In his well-known frank and concrete style, Dr. Danco explores the questions which arise . . . or should arise . . . at each stage in the growth of a family business, the mistakes that are commonly made, and **how they can be minimized or overcome.**

"BEYOND SURVIVAL: A Guide for the Business Owner and his Family" by Léon A. Danco, Ph.D.

. . . for the owner-manager of a successful family business — for the entrepreneur who made it and now wants, somehow, to ensure his dream survives beyond him. In this internationally acclaimed book, Dr. Danco draws **an honest and understanding picture of the business owner and his world:** the who's who of power, how to manage people and money, how to gain commitment from outside advisors, how to manage succession, and how to manage estate planning.

"OUTSIDE DIRECTORS IN THE FAMILY OWNED BUSINESS: Why, When, Who, and How" by Léon A. Danco and Donald J. Jonovic

. . . about working boards of outside directors, and about the family businesses they serve. This book goes point by point through **a concept that has been working effectively in thousands of privately held businesses for more than 20 years.** It is an easy to read, step by step manual for business owners who are concerned with providing a proven way to help assure growth and continuity in their successful family-owned businesses. This is a book about how to change existing boards, how to find and use working outside directors, how to organize and run worthwhile meetings, and about how to live happily with outside directors.

"FROM THE OTHER SIDE OF THE BED: A Woman Looks at Life in the Family Business" by Katy Danco

. . . a book written by, for, and about women in family businesses — wives, ex-wives, wives-to-be, widows, daughters, daughters-in-law, sisters, sisters-in-law, cousins, and owners. Katy Danco, with the help and wisdom of the many women she has met over the past 20 years, has written **a book that helps to answer the important and difficult questions faced by the women who inhabit the fascinating, troublesome world of the successful family business.** Without answers to these and many other questions, it's likely that a family in business just won't succeed.

The Center for Family Business
P.O. Box 24268
Cleveland, Ohio 44124
216/442-0800